THE
CORAL REEF

To Andrea and Luigi,
the sea that brought us together,
my friends, no longer holds any
mysteries for you.

WHITE STAR PUBLISHERS

1 - A classical view of the coral formations of the Australian Great Barrier Reef. This as many other reefs grows in crystal-clear waters above rocky sea bottoms where coral polyps have been reproducing and dying incessantly for thousands of years.

A - A large block of corals is entirely disguised and suffocated by multi-coloured sponges and other filtering organisms, such as small green colonial ascidians (Didemnum sp.). Numerous coloured crinoids and anemones (Heteractis magnifica) can be seen among these with clownfish (Amphiprion nigripes) and black domino damselfish (Dascyllus trimaculatus) hiding amidst their tentacles. The numerous small Anthias (Pseudoanthias squamipinnis) swim alongside the large white tail squirrelfish (Sargocentron caudimaculatum) and triggerfish (Balistapus undulatus).

A

Contents

B

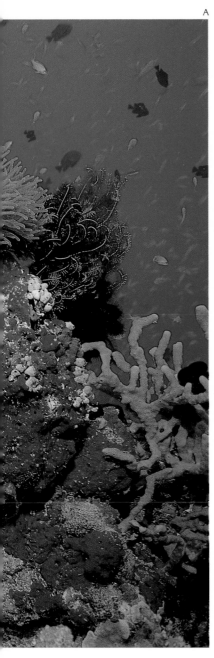

Written by
Angelo Mojetta

Editorial Supervision by
Valeria Manferto De Fabianis
Laura Accomazzo

Graphic Supervision by
Patrizia Balocco Lovisetti

Translation by
Barbara Fisher

© 2003 White Star S.p.A.
Via Candido Sassone, 22-24
13100 Vercelli, Italy
www.whitestar.it

Revised Edition in 2006.

ISBN 10: 88-544-0187-0
ISBN 13: 978-88-544-0187-7

REPRINTS:
2 3 4 5 6 09 08 07 06

Printed in China

B - This atoll of the Maldives is the result of the work of thousands of incredibly small animals that, during the years, have been able to create this fantastic natural prodige.

Cover

The underwater plant life of the Red Sea is abundant.
©Vincenzo Paolillo

Top left
A giant anemone (Condilactys gigantea).
© Roberto Rinaldi

Back cover

Top
*An aerial view
of some atolls
in the Maldives.*
© Kurt Amsler

Center
*An enormous sea fan
stretches its branches.*
© Franco Banfi

Bottom
*The illustration
reconstructs the
subdivision of
habitats on the reef.*
© Franco Banfi

A - What words could be used to summarize the incredible spectrum of sensations stirred at the sight of a reef. Even before being touched and scrutinized these habitats manage to win over the city dweller, overpowering him with the contrasting, sometimes violent, sometimes delicate colours, the ideal backdrop to a new and still little known world.

B - A coral pinnacle rises from the sea bed towards the surface. Standing out from its mass like sculptures are colonies of madrepores ever different in form: cups, bushes, brains, umbrellas. Also the colours differ, pink, yellow and light green contrasting with the bright shades of the fish fluttering around the corals like butterflies.

INTRODUCTION

In an ideal catalogue of the natural wonders on earth a prominent position must be reserved alongside the tropical rain forests, the African savanna and the ices of Antarctica for coral reefs. Warm, crystal-clear waters inviting exploration, exuberant life manifesting itself in a myriad of forms and colours - these are the principal features of the extraordinary habitats peculiar to the tropical regions of our planet, incomparable aquatic environments in equilibrium between the sea and the land and prey to the forces of both. Anyone diving along a coral reef will observe a spectacle comparable only to the lushest equatorial forests. As in that green realm, here in the blue of the ocean man must come to terms with the exceptional variety and vitality of nature.

The human eye loses itself in this fantastic universe as amid the stars in the sky on a clear night in the desert while the shapes of the corals, the multicoloured and often bizarre forms of the fishes and the incessant motion of life reiterating the perpetual rhythm of the waves below the surface all seem destined to remind us in every instant that life originated from the water. Yet, paradoxically, this very apparently inexhaustible life makes it difficult to understand how all can depend on a fragile, surface layer of minute organisms: these madreporitic polyps busy multiplying without respite, untiringly building the limestone skeletons on which to raise their fellows or where other beings will find food and refuge, engaged, as all others, in the never-ending battle for survival.

A

B

500 MILLION YEARS OF HISTORY

Only from an aeroplane or satellite or before elevated fossil reefs is it possible to understand why corals have earned themselves the definitions of "builders of underwater empires" or "architects of the sea".
The many possible examples substantiating this include the Great Barrier Reef in Australia, the coral archipelagos of the Indo-Pacific - where the corals accumulated over thousands of years make life possible for man today - and the many stretches of coasts on the Red Sea where one can stroll amid corals and shells now exposed to the wind and the desert sun. Nor are they exclusive to tropical countries as is shown by fossil corals, very similar to today's species found in the Dolomites, in France, in Great Britain, in Germany and even on the North European island of Gotland (Sweden).
This shows that the history of madreporitic formations and building corals is not recent and

A - The reef of the Bahamas and the deep ocean trench (1300-2000 metres) limiting its boundaries.
The picture taken by the Space Shuttle Endeavour *shows, at the bottom, the fringing reefs surrounding Cuba and, to the left, the island of Andros.*

A

that the first traces of coral reefs date back to approximately 500 million years ago. Between the early Cambrian, the mid Silurian and the mid Devonian epochs (560-360 million years ago) there were at least three periods of considerable worldwide expansion of the corals and of the great carbonatic shelves at the same time as a global rise in temperature and level of the waters, which extended the 20°C mean temperature to latitudes 40-45° N and S. At the moment of maximum expansion, during the Palaeozoic era, experts estimate that, albeit dominated by species with different characteristics from those of today, the coral reefs occupied a surface area of more than 5 million square kilometres and had vertical growth rates of up to 200 metres every million years.

Over a period estimated between 1 and 4 million years during the Famennian (360 million years ago), the reefs were reduced to just over 1000 square kilometres and disappeared almost everywhere. Two principal factors were equally responsible for this rapid collapse

B - The great atoll of Aldabra off the coasts of the Seychelles, northwest of Madagascar, photographed during the flight of Atlantis. For its isolated position the atoll of Aldabra is considered by experts a nature laboratory of the coral ecosystem. Approximately 10% of the fauna and flora found here is endemic. The clear internal lagoon shows the sands accumulated by the sea currents and the channel through which the waters of the ocean mix with those of the lagoon.

and mass extinction of the coral habitats. One was the collision of the ancient supercontinent of Gondwanaland with the north American shield which drastically modified the course of the marine currents; the other was the general reduction in the temperature of the planet.

Since then the great play of plate tectonics, the formation of the oceans, the continental drift, the variations in the sea level and the alternation of glacial periods with others of gradual warming have continued to influence the growth of the barriers in an endless succession of constructions and destructions.

A new development of the coralline formations occurred in the Mesozoic period (approximately 260 million years ago), when great basaltic expansions between India and Pakistan preceded the birth of a new ocean.

The progressive distancing of the great plates and the emission of continuous larva close to the rift valleys led to the formation of an uninterrupted sea, the Tethys, extending from the east westwards and joining the Atlantic, the Mediterranean, the Indian Ocean and the Pacific. Although the environmental conditions were fairly uniform and typically tropical, in faunistic terms, the richest area seems then to have been the Mediterranean. Today this sea is absolutely devoid of reefs but within its confines palaeontologists have identified more than 65 genera of corals, compared with the less than 30 currently present in the whole Atlantic. Towards the end of the Tertiary period, from the Neogene to the Holocene periods (25 million years ago) the fragmentation of the Tethys, caused by continental drifting, led to the formation of the present oceans and had significant consequences on the distribution and evolution of the hermatype corals (from the Greek *erma* = barrier), i.e. those capable of building barriers.

The faunistic pole moved towards the Indo-Malaysian region following the progressive closure of the Mediterranean Tethys when India

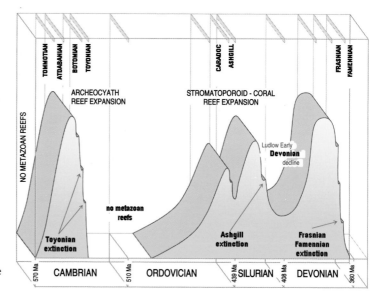

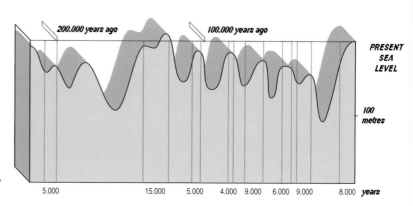

collided with Asia. Subsequently, during the Pliocene epoch (11-14 million years ago) the coralline regions of the western Atlantic also remained isolated from the Indo-Pacific following the gradual advancement and emergence of the lands destined to become Central America. In that far-off period the two main coralline provinces - the Caribbean and the Indo-Pacific - originated.

The corals of the Indo-Pacific underwent a considerable diversification (90 genera) mainly due to evolution within the three basic families: *Acroporidae, Poritidae* and *Pocilloporidae*.

The Caribbean species, in contrast, were reduced (from 40-50 genera to 26) both as a result of isolation following the formation of the

The graph top illustrates the evolution of reefs, their development and disappearance in geographical eras of the past from the Cambrian (570 million years ago) to the Devonian (360 million years ago). The first reefs of the Cambrian period were built by Archaeocyathidae, cup-shaped building organisms having an intermediate biology between that of sponges and true corals. These were followed by reef building organisms just like the madrepores of today.

The graph bottom illustrates the variations in the level of the sea over the last 200,000 years and the periods of growth of coral formations. The red lines separate the phases of active growth from those of stasis or regression. As can be seen, the total period over which corals developed corresponds to slightly more than 30% of the total. Our era comes within an active growth cycle commenced approximately 8000 years ago.

Central American land bridges and for an increase in sedimentation following climatic changes and increased precipitations. Although the history of the evolution of corals and coral reefs appears to have spanned a considerable time, the reefs known today are the result of a small fraction of geological time. They were almost exclusively created by changes in the sea level (transgressions and regressions) consequential to the fusion and solidification of the ices during the interglacial and glacial periods.

During the Pleistocene (approximately 1 million years ago), for instance, the Caribbean region was affected by vertical changes in the average sea level of more than 130 metres. Another wide-ranging variation in the sea level (approximately 120 metres less than at present) also occurred 15,000 years ago, but since then the average level has increased progressively and fairly constantly. Thanks to data obtained from carbon 14 analysis of fossil corals and the study of the growth bands identified in the skeletons of many Madreporaria with the application of gamma ray densitometry, it has been possible to determine that 10,000 years ago the surface of the oceans was only 30 metres lower than today.

The increase in the level of the oceans decreased from 10 m/1000 years to 6 m/1000 years between 10,000 and 7,500 years ago; it further decreased 6000-5000 years ago and even exceeded today's average level between 4000 and 1500 years ago by approximately one metre before stabilizing.

This rise in the seas and oceans had, of course, direct consequences on the growth of corals; a largely vertical type of growth, essential to counteract the rapidly rising waters, was transformed into more horizontal development, favouring the expansion of the reefs.

Data obtained from the study of carrots extracted from the deepest layers of numerous coral reefs in the Caribbean and Indo-Pacific show that the speed of coral growth was rather variable and depended on the region explored, the species considered and the theories followed by the individual experts. For the Great Barrier Reef estimates vary from just over 1 metres to 14 metres every 1000 years, whereas in the Caribbean, for the same time span, the estimated growth of the reefs is between 0.3 and 12 metres.

A

B

C

D

A - From the blue depths of the ocean the coral reefs of the Maldives push up to the surface to form large atolls and lagoons on which break the waves of the open sea.

B - The clear waters of this sheltered bay allow the internal growth of Staghead Acropores in which shoals of blue damselfish take refuge. Even more fascinating is the contrast between the tropical waters and the external landscape where the pine trees are reminiscent of an alpine scene.

C - New Caledonia has a series of reefs at the edge of the Tropic of Capricorn which close a single large lagoon. The great reefs of the past, now emerged, are separated by channels destined to be filled by the growth of new corals. The outer surface, now belonging to the land environment, is colonized by columnar pine trees (Auracaria columnaris), coconut and mangrove trees.

D - The arid desert contrasts with the colours and the wealth of life of the reef before it protected by the waters of the Red Sea. The contrast is even more fascinating as the rocks in the background are made of perfectly identifiable fossil corals.

TODAY'S CORAL FORMATIONS

Today's coralline formations
Ocean geology and palaeontology
provide useful information on the
current distribution of coral reefs.
Moreover, as can be inferred from
a comparison of the genera of
corals present in the various areas,
there would seem to be a regular
gradient of concentration leading
from particularly rich areas (e.g.
the Indo-Pacific area between
Borneo, Celebes, the Philippines
and Papua New Guinea) to poorer
zones. According to many experts
this depends on stable climatic
factors and the coral larvae's

capacity to disperse. The geography
of madreporitic formations shows
how, with rare exceptions, their
growth occurs within the band
between the tropics. In this area,
where they cover more than
600,000 square kilometres^2 equal
to 0.17% of the entire ocean
surface and just under 1/6th of the
coastal strip between 0 and 30
metres (that most suited to the life
of hermatype corals), their
diffusion is not uniform as it is
limited to those areas where the
mean temperature of the water in
winter months is no less than 20°C.
The reason for this limit is easily
understood if one considers that at

*The biology of corals
prevents these
organisms from
settling and growing
in unsuitable
oceanographic
conditions. Sea
currents are one of
the main factors
capable of
influencing coral
distribution. The
comparison
between the
position of reefs
(graph A) and the*

*nature of the
currents shows how
the flow of warm
water (graph C)
allows corals to
grow even beyond
the limits of the
Tropics of Cancer
and Capricorn. In
contrast, cold
currents (graph D)
obstruct or prevent
the growth of reefs
even in
geographically
favourable areas.*

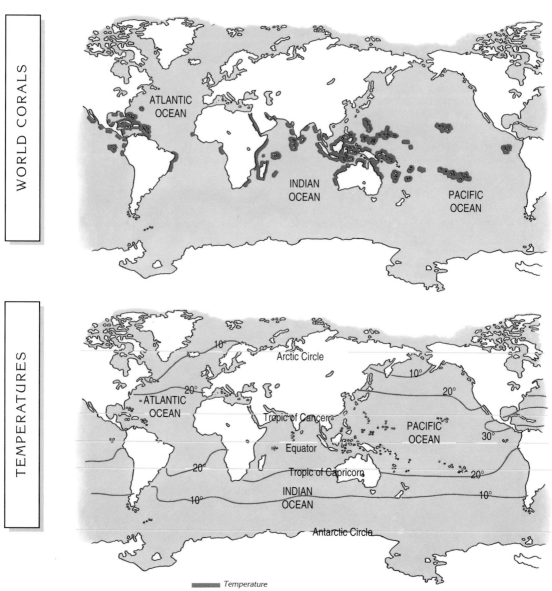

Temperature

18°C. it takes less than two weeks for a colony of *Pocillopora damicornis*, a Madrepora with round section branches common from the Red Sea to Hawaii, to die whereas at 15°C it will die in less than 24 hours. This is but one of the possible examples. The growth of the coralline formations therefore follows the invisible confines marked by the sinuous progress of the isochems, the lines corresponding to the mean winter temperatures indicated above. The leading factor retained essential for the growth of corals is temperature, but this does not mean that reefs cannot be found north and south of the 30° latitudes, the theoretical limits. The extreme confines of the coral empire in the Indo-Pacific lie in Japan and in Australia respectively. In Japan building corals and barriers are found between Kyushu and Shikoku (33° 32' N), at Enourawan (35° 10' N), at Tateyama (35° 10' N), at Kushimoto (33° 25' N) and at Mikaye-Jima (34° 05' N). In Australia the southern limits coincide with the island of Lord Howe (31° 30' S), the Solitary Islands (31° 01' S) and the region of Freemantle (32° S). In the Atlantic the most northern coralline

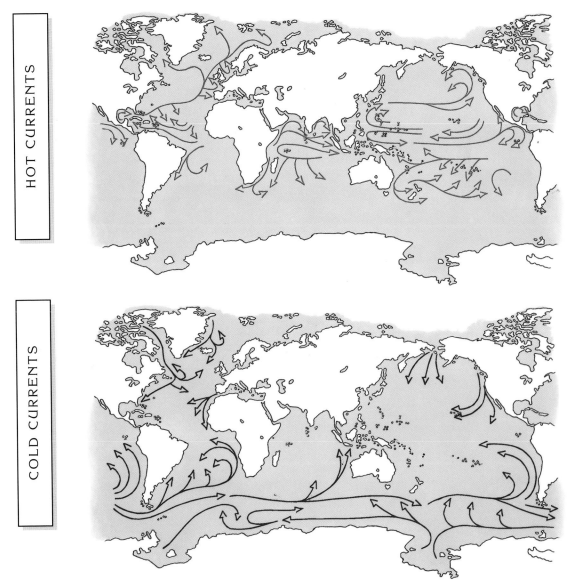

HOT CURRENTS

COLD CURRENTS

11

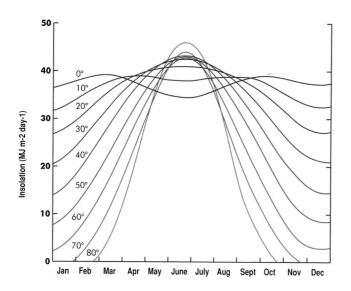

The graph illustrates the variations in solar radiation striking the earth's surface in the course of the year at different latitudes. The variation is extremely small in the intertropical band and this enables corals to benefit from the fairly constant light conditions which favour their growth.

even though most of the species seem capable of tolerating, albeit only for a few hours, salinity values 75% lower than normal.

Thus, violent long or regular rain showers may damage corals, those nearest the surface at least, as the fresh water tends to stratify above the sea water. Even more obvious is the effect of dilution - although this is not the only consequence - attributable to the great rivers (e.g. the Indus, Ganges, Tigris and Euphrates, Orinoco and Amazon); the influx of their waters is such to inhibit all coral growth and constitutes true physical barriers to its expansion even in favourable climatic zones. On the contrary, a high salinity, such as that registered in the Red Sea and the Persian Gulf, is better tolerated by corals. These superior limits cannot be exceeded with impunity: concentrations of 45% are limiting for many species and only some of the *Porites* genus can tolerate a salinity of 48%. The last, though certainly not the least important, of the factors influencing the growth of the barriers is light; this is because of the close dependence that exists, as shall be seen in the next chapter, between this factor and zooxanthellae, symbiont algae contained in the tissue of coralline polyps. These play a fundamental role in the life of the corals by providing them with nourishment and favouring limestone synthesis. As vegetables, zooxanthellae necessarily depend on light to perform photosynthesis and this limits the depth at which they can live and, consequently, also that of the corals. This explains why most reefs are in clear waters and how, on average, their main growth takes place in the first 30 metres, being rapidly reduced beyond this depth. Alongside these main parameters are other minor though not negligible ones which, on a small and medium scale, may considerably influence the distribution and extension of madreporitic constructions. One of these is represented by the tides. Corals cannot tolerate long periods of emersion although the more porous species (e.g. *Porites lutea*)

formations are to be found in the Bermudas (32° 30' N) although two species of building Madrepora are present in Onslow Bay (34° N) on the American coast. The most extreme point south is represented by the barriers growing at the latitude of Rio de Janeiro. Their expansion towards lower latitudes is impeded by the cold current of the Falklands. The fact that, in absolute terms, corals go beyond the theoretical confines assigned to them more frequently northwards than southwards is because the lines coinciding with the average temperatures of the oceans do not run in perfect symmetry with the equator. Generally speaking, higher temperatures are recorded in the northern than in the southern hemisphere. This peculiarity is to be related to the major contact of the three oceans (the Atlantic, Indian and Pacific) with each other in the southern hemisphere and with the Antarctic regions, thus more directly subjected to the influence of very cold water and currents. As we know, the currents are affected by the Coriolis force

caused by the earth's rotation; this deflects them clockwise in the northern hemisphere and anti-clockwise in the southern hemisphere. As a consequence, the masses of ocean water are driven towards or away from the coasts. A clear example of the effects of this complex mechanism is represented by the circulation of the currents in the tropical areas of the Atlantic where the warm surface waters are driven towards the western coasts, richer in corals, and away from the eastern ones of Africa where, despite the favourable latitude, coralline formations are practically absent. The same occurs along the coasts of the Australian continent where, at the same latitude, coral reefs are only present along the eastern coasts. The salinity, i.e. the quantity of salts dissolved in a litre of sea water, is the second factor capable of limiting the distribution of corals. These organisms need water with fairly stable saline concentrations (34-37%, i.e. 34-37 grams of salts per thousand grams of water) and usually suffer with lower values better resist exposure to the air, probably because the numerous furrows in their skeleton favour capillary penetration of the water along the entire colony. Other species can secrete copious amounts of mucous which envelops the colonies, conserving humidity; this is responsible for the formation of surface foam at the time of a flood tide. The direction and force of the winds and the intensity of the wave movement also influence the growth of the reefs. A remarkable formation is that of a coral island 18 kilometres long, 37 metres wide and 3 metres high following the accumulation of material torn from the island of Funafuti (Tuvalu) on 21st October 1972 by the huge waves provoked by the passage of Typhoon Beebe. In other, more frequent, cases the winds blowing constantly towards

the open sea may, close to the coast, cause cold waters to rise from the depths, as is seen in the areas of upwelling (California, Peru) extremely rich in life for the constant influx of nourishing substances. Elsewhere, such as the Andaman region in the southeast Asiatic, reefs grow only in the areas leeward of these islands or in bays protected from the southwest monsoons, whereas on the eastern coasts of the Malaysian peninsula they are located along the western and southwestern coasts protected from the northeastern monsoons. Lastly, in close relation with rainfall and the rivers considered earlier comes the transportation of excessive quantities of sediments into the sea, in bays or gulfs; these suffocate the corals or prevent their settlement at the larva stage.

The graph covers the major coral regions on our planet. The histograms refer to the length in kilometres of the reefs in the area considered. The longest are those in the Philippines (22,450 kilometres) and the least extended (474 kilometres) are along the coasts of Belize.

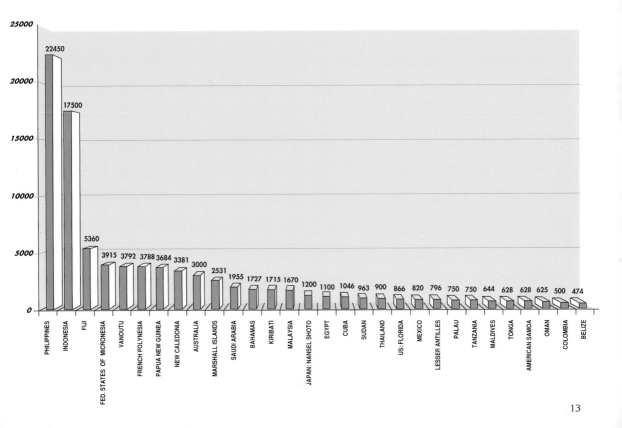

CLASSIFICATION AND DESCRIPTION OF CORAL REEFS

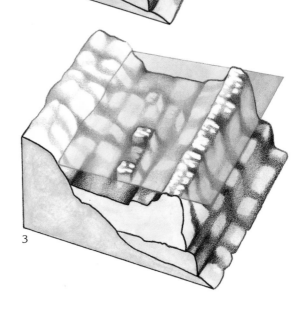

For the widespread distribution of coralline formations, their evolution and the differences existing between them, these coastal, subcoastal and oceanic biological constructions can be ascribed to at least three different categories. On the basis of a classification originating from the studies of Charles Darwin, first expressed in the form of a communication to the *National Geographic Society* in May 1837, and subsequently developed in his book on the structure and distribution of coral banks, it is possible to distinguish fringing reefs, platform reefs and atolls depending on their origin, their form and the relationship they establish with the dry land. The latter two formations in particular, according to substantiated theories, derive respectively from the evolution of a fringing reef rising either over a continental shelf or along the coasts of a volcanic island.

Fringing reefs

Most coastal coral reefs (the Red Sea, Eastern Africa, Persian Gulf, Caribbean) belong to this category although similar reefs are by no means rare close to oceanic islands, provided that the continental shelf does not slope too steeply. They appear as a belt of corals parallel to the shore and with an inner flat reef, facing the coast which may even emerge in parts and an outer reef fronting the open sea. In favourable conditions the belt of corals extends to form a platform which may stretch uninterrupted for some kilometres, although its vertical growth is limited by the range of the tides. The actively growing part fronts the open sea where the environmental conditions (light, oxygenation, concentration of nutrients) are more favourable to the growth of corals. On the inner side the shallow depth brings increases in temperature and salinity, as well as impeding the flow of currents capable of removing the sediments which suffocate the corals.

The three drawings illustrate in sequence the phases leading to the formation of a fringing reef. This type of barrier is considered the most common in the tropical seas.

1) The corals giving origin to a fringing reef settle close to the coast on a rocky substratum.

2) The corals grow gradually towards the open sea leaving behind them an area of coral detritus.

3) In the advanced development phase the fringing reef appears as an inner front facing the coast, a platform at the edge of the tides and an external slope where the madrepores grow actively. The distance from the coast is influenced by the slope of the sea bottom. In some cases wide channels and lagoons with residual reefs form between the reef proper and the coast..

If carefully observed, a fringing reef appears divided, starting from the coastline, into various parts according to the following general pattern. The erosion of the inner front of the reef forms a lagoon between the reef and the coast; this consists in detritus and coral either dead or reduced to sand. Here grow mainly algae or phanerogams (superior plants adapted to aquatic life), rarely do madrepores (e.g. *Favia*, *Porites*, *Platygyra)* manage to establish themselves. At the edges the motion of the waves or the currents erodes the inner profile of the reef, creating baby atolls or pinnacles of madrepores. In part these are still living though considerably eroded but, for this very reason, they can offer countless places of refuge to invertebrates and fish, often the young of the various species. Moreover, coralline algae are frequently capable of growing on branches and broken-off colonies of madrepores, binding them together and offering a further substrate to the filamentous algae which attract shoals of herbivorous fish such as the surgeonfish driven this far during high tide.

Proceeding outwards the reef becomes increasingly compact in line with the belt definable as the internal front. Here the abundance of living forms increases progressively thanks to the influence of the waves which bring nourishment and oxygen and remove the detritus. The inner front is followed by a flat zone, almost a platform, where the conditions of life can be difficult. Here the tides and the waves can be violent and limit growth to the sturdiest of madrepores, such as the brain madrepores, the *Acroporae* or the largest *Favidae*. In contrast, insulation favours the growth of coral or encrusting algae. The hydrodynamics of the water creates corridors, tunnels and craters or kettle-like hollows; these may in time join to create complex labyrinths which can only be explored during high tide, swimming on the surface and in a calm sea. The variety of microhabitats recognizable here is

A - The upper part of the outer margin of a reef, as you can see in this picture taken in Sudan, is edged with waves that break against the corals, capable of growing just below the surface and emerging at intervals. From this point, the highest on the reef, it will grow towards the open sea as far as the light allows the corals to grow actively. Internally a lagoon forms with the accumulation skeletons of dead corals destined to become white coral sand.

B - The Fiji Islands: a chain of coral formations parallel to the coast protects the island from the most violent waves.

C - Fringing barriers are typical of the Red Sea; the image shows the coast close to Nabq. Because deep waters (500-1000 metres) are so close, the corals are short of substrata on which to develop. They grow on dead corals and towards the open sea where conditions are more favourable. The compact reef is interrupted here and there by channels, kept open by the currents.

D - Some coral formations survive in the internal lagoon at Ras Nasrani, Northern Red Sea, but they grow actively at the edges of the deep channel. The lighthouse standing isolated is destined to be ever farther away from the sea it was erected to watch.

A

a prelude for the part of the fringing reef where life is more prolific. The first metres are often dominated, as in the Red Sea, by a remarkable growth of fire corals joined by Madreporaria of the *Favites, Pocillopora, Porites, Goniastrea* and *Montastrea* genera; the crest of the outer reef then falls below the surface, the slope depending on the profile of the sea bed on which the reef has grown. This is the richest part of the reef which may slope gently with a terraced profile, interrupted at intervals by plateaus of coral sand, or plunge almost vertically for hundreds of metres. Branched corals such as staghorn madreporares dominate the most

B

A - The surface platform of the reef where massive corals grow (e.g. Porites, Stylophora, Pocillopora *genera*) is the ideal habitat for herbivores such as surgeonfish of the Acanthurus sohal species.

B - Ramified corals of the Acropora *genus come in an incredible variety of shapes and colours (purple, pink, blue, yellow, green) even within the same species. Ramified acropores are especially plentiful in the upper part of the reef in the less exposed areas, where they offer shelter to myriads of fish and other living organisms.*

C - On the outer slope and in deeper waters corals tend to form wider and flatter colonies which become large umbrellas. These offer shelter to those fish who are not great lovers of light such as red soldierfish (Myripristis murdjan). Swimming above the corals are herbivorous fish e.g. surgeon and damsel fish (Plectroglyphidodon dickii) or carnivores such as Lutjanidae (Lutjanus biguttatus).

C

illuminated band but when light starts to become a limiting factor encrusting corals such as those belonging to the Pectiniidae, Fungiidae and Acroporidae families take over. Gorgonians and soft corals settle in caves and in the shade of the protruding ledges.

D - A pair of butterflyfish (Chaetodon semilarvatus), endemic to the Red Sea, swims at the base of a large colony of unusually shaped Acropora.

E - A large sea anemone hosts a colony of clownfish (Amphiprion sp.).

F - Sturdy massive, pin cushion or meandriform colonies of corals abound in fairly level areas close to the surface. This is a typical adaptation to the greater intensity of the waves and the tides.

G - At this point the outer reef of the Red Sea, close to Hurghada, is dominated by the large umbrella of acropores flanking the soft and fire corals. As generally occurs the wall is animated by the presence of anthias (Pseudanthias squamipinnis), their swaying movements seemingly repeating those of the distant waves.

Platform reefs

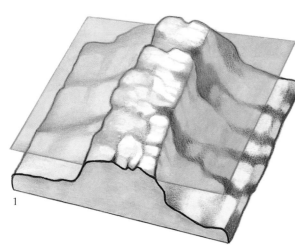

1

are constant is made up of a series of ribbon banks at right angles to the direction of the wind.

Farther south, where the winds are irregular, some banks are perpendicular to the reef line.

Like fringing reefs, platform reefs may also be divided into sections starting from the lagoon.

This usually forms along the side facing the main land or an island and may be dozens of metres deep and hundreds wide.

The inner front, protected from the wave movement, has an intense growth of corals which may be globular and massive, mushroom-shaped or branched and more delicate.

Depending on the local conditions which permitted the initial development of the reef, the sea

Platform reefs develop at varying distances from the coast and even in the open sea if the rocky bottom, generally continental in origin, is close to the surface.

1) Platform reefs start as small fringing reefs.

2) The sea bottom where corals grow tends gradually to sink, increasing the growth of the madrepores upwards and along the inner and external fronts of the reef.

3) During the maximum growth phase - such as for instance in long stretches of the Great Barrier Reef - the platform reef may become a lattice of coral islands and reefs separated by lagoons and channels.

These are coralline formations which again run parallel to the coast but whose growth is considerably superior to that of fringing reefs, as is shown by the Great Barrier Reef, the best known example. Reefs of this kind are also present in Papua-New Guinea, off New Caledonia, in the Fiji Islands and, in the Atlantic, off the coasts of Belize and the Bahamas. This has led some experts to consider these formations as a more advanced stage of development than fringing reefs. Platform reefs grow along the edge of continental shelves and wherever they arrive or are driven to a sufficient distance from the surface to permit the growth of corals.

This means the reefs can grow in all directions and take on the appearance of extended, elongated or oval platforms, or be made up of smaller reefs partially parallel to each other.

The action of the winds, waves and currents can lead to the accumulation of sand in some inner sheltered areas or to the breakage of stretches of reef during the most violent storms, even resulting in the creation of inner channels and lagoons accessible only with small boats. The most northern part of the Australian Barrier Reef, for instance, where the trade-winds

2

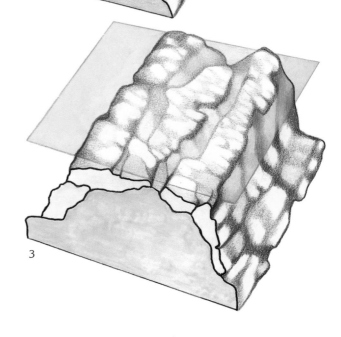

3

A

A - The image taken from the Shuttle shows the northern region of the Bahamas with the islands of Eleuthera, New Providence and Andros. The latter is recognizable on the right for the tidal channels cutting into the coastline. The region of the Bahamas is characterized by deep waters and superficial sandbanks.

B - Part of the Great Barrier Reef stretches along the coasts of Queensland. The light coloured areas of the reef are the sandbanks accumulated along the reef by the southern winds predominant in this area.

B

bottom may appear as a regularly sloping sandbank where the sand alternates with corals forming both extensive banks and vertical pinnacles. The former often originate from broken-off colonies which manage at first to bind themselves together thanks to the action of encrusting algae and then to grow again.

At points where the currents are more intense, the slope may be more accentuated and uneven with the formation of caves, small canyons or terraces which, nonetheless, are always a prelude to stretches of sand.

From here in the direction of the prevailing wave movement, begins a platform-like area stretching possibly for hundreds of metres or more.

This is made up of small corals at the edges of the lagoon; these gradually make way for larger species and surface coralline algae which remain partially uncovered at low tide, allowing a glimpse of the numerous colonies thronging it. Separated by residue pools of water or small channels fish, shellfish and molluscs may remain trapped here.

A

A - The Great Barrier Reef is a collection of reefs with various forms depending on the characteristics of the sea bottom and the oceanographic conditions. This makes the Great Barrier Reef unique and difficult to reduce to a single model.

B - The never-ending battle between the disintegrating action of the tides and the constant growth of the corals gives this section of reef a most varied appearance.
A section of massive reef is flanked by islands or isolated platforms scattered over the area protected by the lagoon. In some stretches of reef there may be hundreds of these mini reefs. The evolution of each one will determine the destiny of the barrier.

B

D

C

C - The compact nature of coral rock and environmental conditions very different from those found on land enable the forces of nature to create bold architectural structures along the steep slopes of the reef. The fantastic substratum allows a countless variety of organisms (sponges, gorgonians, alcyonacea, madrepores, crinoids to mention only the most obvious) to fill each space in a manner only apparently chaotic to our inexpert eyes.

D - A lovely view of the external part of the reef between the surface and the first shelf. In some cases this may extend for hundreds of metres. In other parts it is reduced to a narrow platform beyond which lies the blue sea.

E - The long line of a coral reef stands as a boundary between the great ocean and the stetch of internal sea sheltered by it. Here a lagoon may form with its own characteristic populations.

At the outer edge a crest, very jagged for the breaking of waves, marks the beginning of the coralline wall true and proper; its profile varies from area to area and here the specific difference not only of the corals but of all the other invertebrates and fish reaches a peak, thus rendering any generalization difficult.

E

G - Along the Atlantic coasts of Central America one can dive down to the rocks on which colonies of building corals settled in recent times (at least in geological scale). The sinking of these rocks once emerged was caused by the variations in the level of the sea that occurred here mainly before and after the ice ages.

F

G

F - A diver is exploring an underwater tunnel in New Caledonia. Its dark walls become the ideal habitat for the sciophilous creatures (lovers of shadow) of the reef. Here divers can find organisms typical of deep waters at relatively shallow depths.

H

I

H - The Caribbean: a bluestriped grunt (Haemulon sciurus) near a brain madrepore that has grown close to a large gorgonian.

I - A large colony of staghorn acropores offers refuge to hundreds of Pomacentridae.

Atolls

An atoll is, by definition, a coralline formation encompassing a central circular lagoon; its dimensions can vary from a few kilometres to more than a hundred. These madreporitic constructions are typically found in ocean waters, close to submerged volcanic islands. Only rarely do they grow at the edges of a particularly extensive continental shelf. For their isolation and characteristic form, atolls, more than all other types of coral reefs, have attracted the attention of experts who have focused mainly on trying to explain their origin. Charles Darwin was one of the first to study the formation of atolls and his theory is still the most widely accepted. The explanation given by this great scholar suggests that at the origin of the formation of an

The theory as to the possible mechanism leading to the birth of an atoll was put forward by Charles Darwin and has remained basically valid to this day.

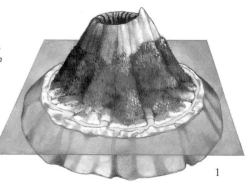

1

1) An atoll originates from fringing reefs surrounding the coast of a volcanic island.

2) Slowly the island starts to subside and the belt of corals becomes increasingly wider and more compact.

3) The island, now almost disappeared, is surrounded by a ring of corals defining a crown of deep waters.

atoll were a series of fringing reefs established in the shallow rocky waters surrounding an elevated volcanic island. The gradual lowering of the substrate following subsidence phenomena permitted the coralline formations to increase in thickness and to evolve into a continuous reef which, after the complete submersion of the island, eventually encircled a lagoon. Darwin's theory, in the absence of today's perfected instruments, based solely on attentive

observation and clever deductions has nonetheless been effectively confirmed. The deep boring carried out in 1951 on the atoll of Eniwetok, at 1267 and 1405 metres led to the identification of an uninterrupted layer of corals, the deepest being a fossil species dating from the Eocene epoch (49-50 million years ago). Knowledge of the biology of the Madreporaria made it immediately impossible to believe that these organisms had developed at such

depths and grown upwards; it was thus clear that their presence so far from the surface could only be explained by subsidence of the sea bottom. More recent oceanographic exploration conducted in the northern Pacific, from Hawaii towards the peninsula of Kamchatka, has shown the existence of an ideal boundary at approximately 28° N called Darwin Point; beyond this there are only submerged volcanic cones, so-called guyots, topped by atolls with a flat surface. Underwater

2

3

4) The island has disappeared. The belt of corals is fully developed and defines a deep lagoon communicating with the outside sea thanks to channels kept open by violent sea currents.

5) The combined effect of the currents, waves and tides plus the growth of the corals modifies the emerged part of the atoll which may rise some metres above the surface forming - sometimes large - islands.

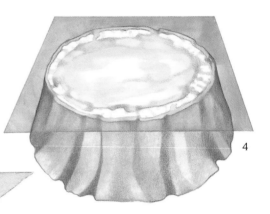

4

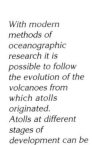

5

With modern methods of oceanographic research it is possible to follow the evolution of the volcanoes from which atolls originated. Atolls at different stages of development can be identified along an imaginary line stretching from the Hawaiis, rich in volcanoes, to the coasts of the Kamchatka peninsula. The volcanic islands move slowly northwards following the movements of the Pacific plate. The islands gradually sink giving origin to atolls; the building corals on these remain active to 28° north. This latitude coincides with the so-called Darwin's Point; beyond this corals cease to grow and, as a result of subsidence, the atolls become guyots, extinct submerged volcanoes destined to disappear in millions of years for the effects of the movement of the oceanic plates.

A

B

C

D

A - The picture shows the three main volcanoes of the Hawaiis: Mauna Loa (in the background), Mauna Kea (centre) and Kilauea (right), still active.

B - A deep wide channel separates two vast atolls in the Maldives archipelago.

surveys have revealed the presence of a regular series of guyots at increasing depths in the direction of the Kamchatka trench, a continuation of the volcanic islands and atolls originating from a point of intense volcanic activity situated at 15° +/- 4° N. As a result of the tectonic movements of the Pacific plate, volcanic islands and atolls are carried north-westwards and gradually sink. The presence of flat coralline formations on the top of the guyots must, in turn, be linked with the gradual slowing down in the limestone production of the corals, caused by the decrease in temperature which favoured erosion rather than bioconstruction.

As well as Darwin's theory, we must mention that of Penck and Daly developed between the end of the last century and the beginning of this one. These two scholars, respectively a geographer and a geologist, claimed that the principal cause of the formation of the atolls lay in the variations in the sea level rather than the subsidence of the islands. Experts currently believe both theories to be valid as they have been proven to be complementary. An atoll, like the aforementioned reefs, can present zonation. The centre consists in a lagoon; in some cases this may reach

E - The coast of Moorea, in French Polinesia, is surrounded by an almost uninterrupted fringing reef. The subsidence phenomena typical of this geographical area will, in thousands of years, lead to the diasappearance of the central island, a lagoon encompassed by an atoll appearing in its place.

F - The large internal lagoon of Bora-Bora occupies a space once filled by a crater. The gradual sinking of the volcanic island increased the thickness of the corals of the surrounding reefs. As can be imagined the process is still in course and it will take thousands of years before the volcanic island yields its place entirely to a coral atoll.

several dozen metres in depth, the bottom not necessarily being sandy and populated by algae. If the transparency of the waters and the currents allow a regular vivification, large coralline formations can be found, however isolated, or pinnacles created by the erosion of ancient madreporitic masses always an attraction for invertebrates and fish. Often the central lagoon is separated by a sandy ridge from an outer lagoon adjoining the reef leeward.
The appearance of the reef surrounding the lagoon, on the other hand, depends on the exposure to the winds. The side where these blow most strongly is generally higher and may, for the accumulation of coralline sand and detritus, give rise to islands capable of hosting a fair vegetable covering of plants grown from seeds arrived by natural means, carried by the currents, the wind, birds or man. Their survival and the luxuriant growth often manifested never cease to amaze those approaching these paradises

E

F

G

where no trace of fresh water is to be found. In actual fact there is water but it is limited to a deep watertable; the water penetrates this during rainfalls but, because of the difference in salinity between the two liquids, remains without mixing with the salts impregnating the subsoil or the sea water.
It then rises again to the surface by capillary flow.

H

G - This group of clams may originate from larvae carried here by the currents or be the result of the violent sea-storm that tore away the block of corals and dragged it inside the lagoon.

H - The corals scattered around the lagoon lead a highly precarious existence. An abundance of sediment and the warming of the waters are serious obstacles to their survival.

CORAL GEOGRAPHY

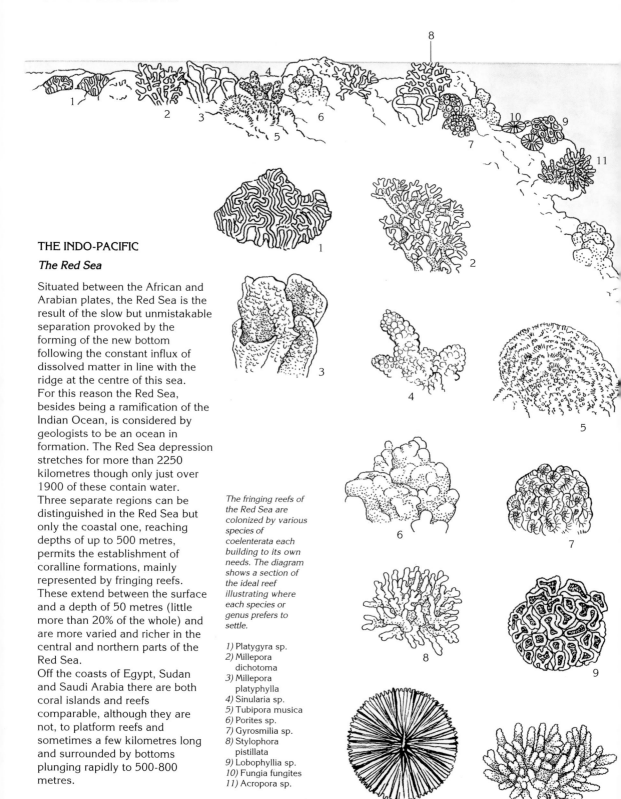

THE INDO-PACIFIC

The Red Sea

Situated between the African and Arabian plates, the Red Sea is the result of the slow but unmistakable separation provoked by the forming of the new bottom following the constant influx of dissolved matter in line with the ridge at the centre of this sea. For this reason the Red Sea, besides being a ramification of the Indian Ocean, is considered by geologists to be an ocean in formation. The Red Sea depression stretches for more than 2250 kilometres though only just over 1900 of these contain water. Three separate regions can be distinguished in the Red Sea but only the coastal one, reaching depths of up to 500 metres, permits the establishment of coralline formations, mainly represented by fringing reefs. These extend between the surface and a depth of 50 metres (little more than 20% of the whole) and are more varied and richer in the central and northern parts of the Red Sea.

Off the coasts of Egypt, Sudan and Saudi Arabia there are both coral islands and reefs comparable, although they are not, to platform reefs and sometimes a few kilometres long and surrounded by bottoms plunging rapidly to 500-800 metres.

The fringing reefs of the Red Sea are colonized by various species of coelenterata each building to its own needs. The diagram shows a section of the ideal reef illustrating where each species or genus prefers to settle.

1) Platygyra sp.
2) Millepora dichotoma
3) Millepora platyphylla
4) Sinularia sp.
5) Tubipora musica
6) Porites sp.
7) Gyrosmilia sp.
8) Stylophora pistillata
9) Lobophyllia sp.
10) Fungia fungites
11) Acropora sp.

A - This picture taken during the Apollo 17 mission, clearly defines the Red Sea set between Africa and Asia, the Mediterranean and the Indian Ocean.

B - The deepest and less illuminated points of the reef are colonized preferably by organisms not very fond of light such as soft corals.

C - Along the reef the currents are more regular and large fans of gorgonians (Subergorgia hicksoni) grow.

D - The emerged platform reaching out to the sea is made up of the same corals that are still building the reef around Shadwan. The fall in the level of the sea has uncovered the ancient reef transforming it into rock.

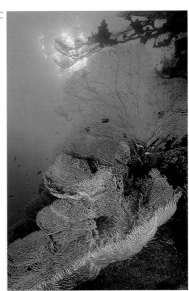

A

B

D

E

E - A typical coral shoal surrounding a low island in the Red Sea.

The western coasts of the Indian Ocean

Separated from each other by deep trenches, the coralline areas of the western Indian Ocean are particularly well-developed along the coasts of the African continent, especially Kenya and Tanzania with branches extending as far as Somalia where, despite the relative proximity of the Red Sea, cold water rising from the deeps prevents the growth of comparable corals. Better known are the coralline beds of the numerous islands which represent the peaks of the underwater chains running along the Indian Ocean bottom. Outstanding among these for its

B

A - A satellite view of the archipelago of the Maldives. Part of the archipelago consists in small coral atolls called faros by the locals; these grow close to each other forming rings - some reaching hundreds of kilometres long - around a lagoon.

A

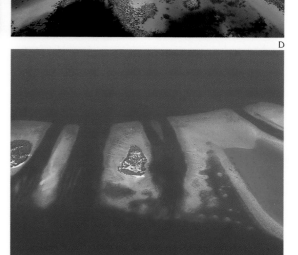

C

D

B, C - The mini atolls of the Maldives generally consist in a coral island with vegetation in front of a lagoon closed by a reef.

D - In this aerial view of the Maldives can be clearly seen lagoons, passes and fringing reefs.

size is Madagascar, a continental island surrounded north and south by fringing reefs. To the north are the Seychelles, an archipelago composed of more than 40 main islands rising from the vast bank of the same name, less than 60 metres deep whereas the surrounding ocean plunges to 4000-5000 metres.

Originating from the Precambrian period (approximately 650 million years ago), the Seychelles are mainly of granite, therefore of continental type rock, to such a degree that they are on the whole considered a microcontinent isolated when the Indian Ocean formed. Fringing reefs are particularly well developed along the coasts of Mahé and Praslin. Southwest of the Seychelles are the atolls of the Amirante islands. The underwater ridge extends

E

southwards, emerging at intervals at the Coetivy, Agalega, Tromelin, Providence, Farquhar, Cargados, Carajos and Rodrigues islands with their tabular reefs. The final part of the underwater ridge are the Mascarene islands with the volcanic islands of Réunion, still active, and Mauritius where the now extinct volcano has allowed a considerable growth of coralline formations.

As one reascends towards the Indian subcontinent the number of coralline formations decreases. The general conditions of the southern coasts of the Arabian peninsula, much of the Persian Gulf and the coasts of Pakistan and of the Arabian Sea are considerably affected by the influx of fresh water and sediment carried by the Tigris, Euphrates and the great river Indus as too by the oxygen-starved cold water rising from the deeps during the southwest monsoon.

Not until much farther south, where the 2000 kilometre ridge of the Maldives starts do coralline

E -The reef walls, turned towards the wide channels dividing the atolls from each other, plunge down into the blue with a steep slope, home to numerous soft corals.

*F - The deepest and least illuminated parts of a reef are chosen by organisms not very fond of the light e.g. the black sea whip corals (*Cirripathes sp.*) and the Hydrozoa of the* Distichopora *genus which form red-orange fans with white tips.*

F

A

A - A small green island emerges from a coral shoal in the Seychelles.

B - The most superficial coral formations of the Maldives are rich in species forming large ramified or platform colonies such as the acropores or sturdy finger-shaped structures such as Porites.

formations appear. Those farthest north belong to the Laccadive islands: on this archipelago the coralline formations change gradually from platform reefs to atolls (e.g. those of Kavaratti, Kalpeni and Minikoy, the southernmost of the Laccadive islands) characterized by shallow lagoons. The ridge continues with the elevated summits of the peaks on which the Maldives stand, an archipelago of more than a thousand islands, some still in formation, and stretching for 800 kilometres. Atolls are the

B

D

C

C - A flat sea bottom dominated by currents close to the coast of Réunion. At the centre is a giant anemone occupied by a pair of Amphiprion clarkii.

Peeping out from a shaded crevice is a small grouper, rising in the background are the threadlike contours of sea whip gorgonians (Junceella sp.).

D - The submerged volcanic rocks of the island of Réunion are poor in coral formations although the

scenery can be equally fascinating, such as this arch framing a large gorgonian twisted by the currents.

predominant coralline formations, especially in the south of the archipelago. It is no chance that the highly familiar word atoll should come from the Maldivian word *atholu* meaning "islands in a ring"; it was introduced into Europe by a certain Tyrard, a Frenchman who lived on these islands in the 17th century.
A perfect example, one of the best

F

G

E - A mixed shoal of Plectorhinchus orientalis identified by their spotted fins and Lutjanus kasmira with its characteristic horizontal blue stripes.

F - A coral wall scattered with tabular corals, an adaptation to the poor light, and large sea anemones offering refuge to numerous clownfish (Amphiprion akallopsis).

G - A shoal of carangids (Caranx sexfasciatus) on the sea bed at Aldabra, an isolated atoll where the last giant turtles of the Testudo gigantea species survive.

known atolls, Suvadiva, is situated at the southernmost extremity of the archipelago and is 35 kilometres wide and 70 kilometres long. Prevalent in the northern part of the Maldives, on the other hand, are annular coralline formations interrupted by stretches of sea. The natives call these formations *faros* and the internal lagoons *velu*. The ridge ends beyond the equator with the island of Diego Garcia coming after the Chagos archipelago, small coralline islands emerging from a bank which underwater exploration has shown to be similar to a giant submerged atoll with margins arriving 10-20 metres from the surface.
To the east there is an approximate repetition of the situation found in the Arabian Sea. The flow of the large rivers like the Ganges and the Irrawaddy into the vast Bay of Bengal prevents the growth of corals. These appear farther south with the fringing barriers of the Andaman and Nicobar islands, whose curve of mountainous peaks testifies to ancient links with continental Asia. Not far from the coasts of Thailand are some of the best known diving areas: Phuket island, the Similans and the lesser known archipelago of Phi Phi Don. Sumatra and Java are, in turn, surrounded by various types of coralline formations.

H

H - The archipelago of the Seychelles is singular within the spectrum of "coral" islands. They are granitic islands of continental origin *and are the highest part of a vast bank approximately 60 metres deep rising steeply from depths of more than 4000 metres.*

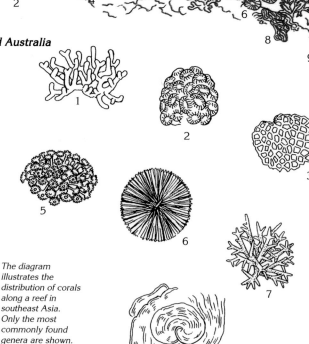

Between Asia and Australia

1
2
3
4
5
6
7
8
9
10
11
12
13

A

The diagram illustrates the distribution of corals along a reef in southeast Asia. Only the most commonly found genera are shown.

Southeast Asia includes the Malaysian archipelago, Borneo, Celebes, the Philippines, the islands of southern Japan and the distant Moluccas. This is a large area where the relatively shallow waters favour the development of all types of coastal formations: fringing reefs, platform reefs, but also atolls. As can be seen from the pages of a reasonably detailed atlas, the Java, Flores, Banda, Celebes, Molucca and Sulu seas succeed each other in a complex weave of "Mediterranean" seas surrounded by islands and archipelagos - altogether this is one of the richest areas of life in the whole Indo-Pacific. Here more than 500 coral species can be found as well as more than 3000 fish species, a third of these being endemic.

Surface corals:
1) Porites sp.
2) Favia sp.
3) Favites sp.
4) Goniastrea sp.

Outer reef margin:
5) Goniopora sp.
6) Fungia sp.
7) Acropora sp.
8) Platygyra sp.

Outer and deep slope of the reef:
9) Pachyseris sp.
10) Lobophyllia sp.
11) Tubastrea sp.
12) Turbinaria sp.
13) Heliopora sp.

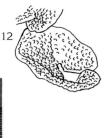

B

A - A seabed rich in soft corals. At the centre a Sarcophyton; at the bottom a Sinularia.

B - Situated at the centre of a triangle capped by the Philippines, Borneo and New Guinea, the archipelago of

the island of Sulawesi is surrounded by more than 15,000 square kilometres of coral reefs.

C

The Great Barrier Reef

A paragraph apart must be dedicated to the Great Barrier Reef of Australia. Starting from the Torres Strait, beyond which corals cannot grow for the constant influx of sediments and fresh water from the Fly river descending from the mountainous chains of New Guinea, this extends southwards along the coasts of Queensland for approx. 2000 kilometres, covering a surface area of 200,000 square kilometres to Lady Elliot Island, its southernmost point. Such a vast extension makes it easy to understand how limiting the term "barrier" is as a traveller will find before him a mixture of fringing reefs, platforms, islands and coralline banks. In the south near the Heron and Capricorn (now a marine park) islands and Wistaria Reef, the coast is less than 100 kilometres away, but suffice to cross less than half this distance to encounter the first coralline habitats represented by isolated ribbon and fringing reefs. Proceeding northwards the width of what is called the Great Australia Channel(a sort of marine motorway permitting navigation without instruments between coast and corals) increases as too does the extension of the reef to reach 20 kilometres. The distance from the coast and the width of the reef have caused the tides and the currents to create a thick weave of channels and lagoons where conditions are ideal for coral growth thanks to a constant influx of nourishment and changing water. In the centre, in the strip roughly between Townsville and Cairns, the Reef appears especially close, thanks partly to the shallow depths where the corals form thin scattered reefs with few islands and numerous small lagoons. Beyond this protected strip the slow

C - Black volcanic rocks bear witness to the violence of the phenomena that gave birth to these coasts. In thousands of years water has overcome fire; lush vegetation flourishes externally and coral gardens stretch out below the surface of the sea.

D

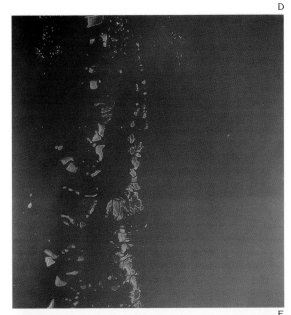

D - A satellite picture of the southern part (Swain Reef) of the Australian Barrier Reef.

E - Heron Island is one of the best known resorts on the Australian Great Barrier Reef, lying approx. 70 km from the coast. Visible at the top are the small tourist resort and the channel providing access through the reef. This artificial channel has caused serious problems of erosion on the coast because of the increased intensity of the tidal currents.

F - This aerial photograph allows an appreciation of the size of the Australian reef and the reason why it was so feared by ancient seafarers, forced to sail along it for days on end in the hope of finding a passage giving access to the coast or back to the open sea.

G - A shoal of snappers (Lutjanus adetti). By day these fish gather around corals and rocky pinnacles.

E

F

G

33

subsidence of the continental shelf has allowed more distant and larger reefs to form, such as those of Holmes and Flinders or Dart and Lihou, the latter now marine parks. The northern part is probably the richest and most spectacular. Less than 50 kilometres from the coast (16 kilometres at Cape Melville) the reef fully deserves its name as it forms an almost unbroken dam of ribbon coralline formations, sometimes 20 kilometres long, rising at the edges of deep oceanic waters and interrupted only by narrow passages. As in the case of the Providential Channel, the names of these convey the joy experienced on their sighting by the sailors of times gone by, afraid of remaining imprisoned for ever and being shipwrecked in the narrow channel between the reef and the coast.

A

B

A - Although classified as a single structure, the Great Barrier Reef is actually a belt of reefs, islands and channels alternating to create ever changing and complex geometric structures.

B - A coral beach has formed in the shelter of an emerged reef.

C - A diver is observing a large madrepore formation, that has grown in the waters of Heron Island.

D - The orderly arrangement of these umbrella madrepores allows every colony to receive the quantity of solar energy most suited to the life of its symbiont algae.

C

D

E

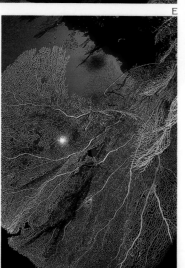

E - The light of a diver's torch shows clearly the delicate structures of a large fan gorgonian, which has grown along the walls of a reef in the Coral Sea.

The western, central and eastern Pacific

The western Pacific includes the vast region stretching from the Solomon Islands and the New Hebrides as far as the Fiji Islands and the Tonga archipelago. The sea bottom is characterized by deep trenches and ridges marking the basins occupied by islands and archipelagos, remains of the bridge of land which joined Australia, New Guinea and New Caledonia and sometimes grouped under the name of Melanesia. Atolls are rare in this area with fringing and platform reefs being more common. The latter are particularly well developed along the western and eastern coasts of New Caledonia parallel to which rise the Loyalty Islands. To the east stretch the Fiji Islands, volcanic in origin, marked by coralline reefs to the north-west and various formations in the remaining part of the archipelago, where one can dive along fringing reefs, coralline islets lush with vegetation, quasi-

F

G

H

I

F - Tiny and practically uninhabited, the Palau Islands are joined by coral formations and separated by deep channels where encrusting organisms create wonderful, highly coloured frescoes.

G - Reefs and atolls are to be found in the Fiji Islands, volcanic islands of the Central Pacific. In the image it is possible to see a channel that goes from the lagoon to the open sea.

H - This aerial picture shows some small atolls in formation in the Pacific Ocean, close to the Philippines.

I - The danger presented by reefs in many parts of the Pacific is demonstrated by the presence of lighthouses, often the only trace of mankind for hundreds of miles.

atolls and atolls proper.
The Tonga, Samoa and Cook islands are continental whereas the Society Islands are typically volcanic. The latter, together with the Tuamotu, Gambier, Tubuai and Marquesas islands form the so-called Polynesia, a collection of approx. 120 islands with a total area of 4000 square kilometres scattered over a section of the ocean as large as Europe. These include forty or so volcanic islands, recognizable both for their massive form and their height (the highest reaches 2237 metres) as well as for the black sand of their beaches; the remainder are typically coralline and only just reach 3-5 metres above sea level. Most are edged with coralline formations of varying dimensions and importance. Reefs are absent from the Marquesas Islands but present alongside the fringing reefs in the Gambier and Society islands.
The atolls of the latter show various degrees of development depending on the island considered. Bora-Bora is considered a quasi-atoll with only the peak of the volcanic

A

B

encrusting algae. There are, nonetheless, a great number of fringing reefs, platform reefs and atolls. The first dominate on the coasts leeward from Hawaii, Maui, Molokai, Oahu and Kauai. Platform reefs are more numerous in the leeward Hawaiian islands, while the best known atolls include Midway, Pearl, Hermes and Kure, the northernmost atoll in the whole Pacific.

The eastern Pacific appears a marginal area in the biogeography of coralline formations. Separated by more than 4000 kilometres of deep waters from the coralline areas of the central Pacific, this region has suffered from its isolation and evolutionary history.

A - New Caledonia: The coral beds can be clearly seen from the air and from the lagoon..

B - A large block of coral has grown in the lagoon in front of Pine Island, in New Caledonia.

C - The great reef of New Caledonia. The atolls in the background are separated by deep channels where the strong tidal currents dominate.

D - A diver exploring a reef colonized mainly by one coral in the Pacific seabeds.

mountain emerging. The outer margin of its lagoon is now made up of coral islands rich in vegetation similar to those seen at Tetiaroa. The situation of Moorea is, however, different; the now extinct volcanic cone is furrowed by valleys ending in bays, deeply indented and transformed into lagoons protected from the waves by fringing reefs. The volcanic cone of Huahine, although large and still elevated, is surrounded by almost unbroken reefs. Typical of these cliffs is the presence, generally windward, of deep channels, called *hoa*; these assure the revitalization of the internal lagoon and communications with the open sea thanks to the violent currents formed with the tides. Particularly well-developed are the more than 80 atolls of the Tuamotu Archipelago where (at Rangiroa) the second largest atoll of the central Pacific is to be found, the largest (100 kilometres wide) being at Kwajalein, in the Ralik chain to the east of the Marshall Islands. A description of the coralline regions of the Pacific would not be complete without a mention of the Hawaiian islands. Situated on the edge of the tropical band and aligned from north-west to south-east by the eastern drift of the Pacific plate, these islands appear poorer in fauna and corals than the areas thus far described, so much so that in certain areas the reefs consist mainly in

C

D

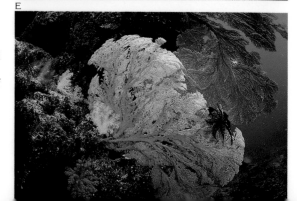

E

The principal madreporitic constructions are found along the coasts of central America where they are mainly represented by fringing barriers. The best known are found in the Chiriqui Gulf in Panama and near Gorgona Island in Colombia. Formations are also reported at El Pulmo Reef (Baja California), in the gulf of Papagayo, in the Panama Gulf (Contadora Island) and in the so-called Golfito (Costa Rica). Parallel to the coast lies a series of islands, elevated parts of a long ridge, such as the Revillagigedo, Cocos and Malpelo islands - the perfect prelude to the Galapagos Archipelago.

Despite the fact that they straddle the equator, these are the southernmost point at which corals can still grow (only about twenty species) in the eastern Pacific because of the influence of the cold Peru Current.

G

H

F

I

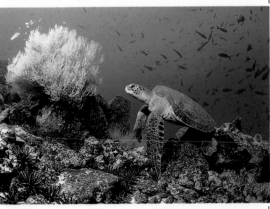

J

E - An expanse of gorgonians (Subergorgia mollis) on the sea bed of Noumea Island. Highly coloured, ethereal, almost as if made of glass, soft corals (Alcyonacea order) like Gorgonians belong to the class of Octocorals. This means that their polyps have 8 feathery tentacles.

F - Delicate seastar are lying on the flat seabottom of the Galapagos.

G - This general view let you observe a number of small islands close to Bora Bora; a rich vegetation has grown on the islands creating a vivid colour contrast.

H - The Galapagos Islands are practically at the limits of the coral domain. Their isolated position and the oceanographic conditions make these islands an experimental nature laboratory also below the surface of the waves; warm and cold waters mix here allowing both corals and penguins to thrive.

I - A green turtle swims above the reef, where you can observe delicate orinoids and large coral formations.

J - This image shows the rich fauna that populates the Galapagos: a group of seals (Zalophus californianus), is posing for the photographer.

The Atlantic

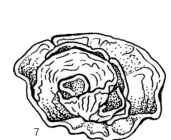

The Caribbean measures approximately 800 kilometres wide and is about 2000 long, a relatively modest area if compared with that of the Pacific but dominated by the Caribbean current flowing from east to west and by a coastal counter-current which together create numerous internal vortexes. Considering that many of the organisms in this area have planktonic larvae capable of surviving for long periods in the open sea before settling, it is easy to understand the reason for the relatively uniform fauna of this area, stretching practically from the northern coasts of South America to Florida, the Bahamas and the Bermudas.
This northern archipelago lies just over 1000 kilometres from the coasts of the United States and can be considered an outpost of the Caribbean which owes its survival to the influence of the Gulf Stream. Coralline formations are also to be found along the coasts of Texas and, above all, Florida, from Dry Tortugas to Key Largo.
To the east of the Florida trench stretches a vast platform of fossil corals, which extends to form the banks of the Bahamas, consisting in more than 3000 islands, *cays* (small semi-submerged formations partly of coralline origin and partly the result of organogenic bonding of sand and detritus) and elevated

rocky banks lying on a platform surrounded by deeper waters. Particularly interesting for its grottoes and blue holes is the island of Andros, on the edge of a depression more than 4000 metres deep. The favourable conditions of the bottom have allowed the development of the second largest reef in the western Atlantic.
The West Indies, i.e. the Greater and Lesser Antilles, form a long curve of islands stretching from Cuba to Aruba. Here, the growth of coralline formations is considerably influenced by the presence of suitable rocky substrates and the climatic

The diagram illustrates the arrangement of the various forms of corals along a reef in the Caribbean.

1) Staghorn coral (Acropora cervicornis)
2) Fragments and broken colonies of A.cervicornis.
3) Elkhorn coral (Acropora palmata)
4) Fragments and broken pieces of Elkhorn coral (Acropora Palmata) colonies.
5-6) Rock corals (Montastrea sp.)
7) Lettuce corals (Agaricida sp.)

38

conditions. The islands and usually the coasts facing the Caribbean Sea are more protected and the rich sea bottoms of Cuba, Hispaniola and Puerto Rico are characterized by well developed fringing reefs. Curiously, as this coralline formation is practically unknown in the Atlantic, to the north of the eastern tip of Cuba there is a small atoll called Reef Hogsty. On the coastal side fronting the Atlantic, the Lesser Antilles in particular, the bottom is not so rich although it does improve along the coasts of the Dutch Antilles, Bonaire, Curaçao and Aruba, famous for having been the backdrop for the first underwater explorations conducted by Hans Hass.

Although protected from the direct

influence of the Atlantic by the Greater Antilles, Jamaica and the Cayman Islands lie close to relatively deep waters. This allows the formation of lush reefs though it does limit growth out to sea, creating steep walls which rapidly plunge to 50 metres and more. The barrier reefs protecting the coasts of Central America are well-developed. Of particular interest are those fronting Belize for more than 250 kilometres, considered the second largest coral reef in the world after that of Australia.

A phenomenon typical of this area are the huge "blue holes" such as that opening at the centre of Lighthouse Reef, a deep blue chasm, what remains of an emergent cavern opening in the soft blue of the surrounding sea and plunging vertically to 125 metres. Decidedly poorer, perhaps for the influx of cold waters rising periodically from the bottom, are the coralline beds of Venezuela (archipelago of Los Roques) which represent the last but one outpost of the American Reefs.

Their growth impeded by the great mass of fresh water flowing into the

A - This picture taken from the camera on the Shuttle after the passage of hurricane Andrew, on 24 August 1992, shows the southern Florida; a part of Florida Keys, extending toward Cuba, is just visible at the bottom of the photo.

B

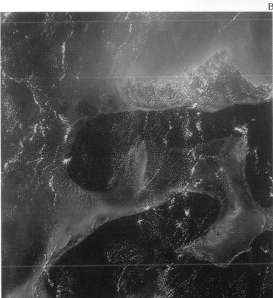

B - The Bahamas Bank seen from the satellite reveals its complex topography. The light coloured areas may be less than 3 metres deep, the dark blue parts plunge to depths of more than 2000 metres.

C

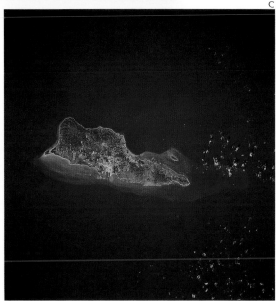

C - The island of St. Croix in the Virgin Islands is surrounded by reefs in the eastern area. These reefs and the small island make up the National Marine Park of Buck Island.

A - A small island in Martinique has a salt water lagoon. Around the land stripe, a rich vegetation has developed and white sand beaches go toward the deep blue of the ocean.

B - The picture shows the island of Petite Terre in Guadalupe. The distribution of the coral formations along these islands in the Caribbean Atlantic is influenced by the coasts. The reefs, in turn, protect the islands from the violence of the breakers, permitting the development of beaches and vegetation.

sea from the mouths of the Orinoco and the Amazon rivers and the sediments that these contain, barrier reefs reappear only after Capo São Roque to arrive as far as Rio de Janeiro.

These are, nonetheless, fringing reefs or more limited formations, only partly composed of corals and more similar to large rocky masses. Most of the constructing organisms are represented here by coralline and encrusting algae and sedentary animals with a limestone skeleton.

Off Cape Sao Roque, the island of Fernando di Noronha, with sparse madreporitic formations despite the transparency of its waters, seems almost to announce the

C - The violence of the waves interferes with the growth of the corals which only develop in the most sheltered areas of Pointe des Chateaux, Guadalupe.

D

D - The contrasting colours at Cayo Largo, Cuba, reveal the different depths between one point and another, in this area varying from 6 to 60 metres. The depths surrounding this resort not far from the main island are famous for the abundance of lobsters.

H

E

E - The white beaches of Caneel Bay, a stretch of coast on St. John, one of the American Virgin Islands, have developed at points marked by dominating currents and winds, with the accumulation of coral sediment on the surface.

F - The Caribbean waters are characterized by the presence of a considerable variety of gorgonians. The photograph shows a number of Gorgonia flabellum, known as the fan of Venus.

G - The Grenadines: the corals settle at the edge of the rocky shoals surrounding the four small islands, creating an almost uninterrupted barrier. Inside lagoons form, and other coral formations may grow parallel to the currents caused by the alternation of high and low tides.

F

G

distant islands of Cape Verde, where the only coralline formations worthy of this name in the western Atlantic can be found, even though they have few more than five coral species and are a pale reflection of the far more luxuriant madreporitic formations of the Caribbean and Indo-Pacific.

H - A tidal channel divides the reef growing along this stretch of coast in Honduras allowing the ocean water to give life to the internal side of the reef.

CORAL BIOLOGY

A - The flexibility of the large fans of the Gorgonians (Gorgonacea order) stems from the low calcification of their skeletons, the rigid part consisting mainly in corneal matter. These colonial invertebrates differ from reef-building corals in that their polyps have eight feathery tentacles (not six).

B - A rigid skeleton and ramified structure make fire corals very similar to real corals. The resemblance is, however, only virtual. Fire corals belong to the class of Hydrozoa and are more closely related to Jelly-fishes. They have a remarkable stinging capacity thanks to the nematocysts of the polyps. These are specialized in the defence of the colony and protrude from tiny pores dotted over the surface of the fire coral branches. It is no mere coincidence that these organisms were given the name of Millepores.

C - Madrepores and "non Madrepores" (fire corals, Gorgonians, soft and black corals) congregate, overlap and succeed one another on coral reefs, enriching them with often bright colours and extraordinary forms, incredible differences being found within a single systematic group.

The term coral, as it is commonly intended by divers and enthusiasts, lends itself to numerous misunderstandings in strictly zoological and scientific terms. This happens mainly because the many books on these extraordinary organisms broadly use the word coral to describe all creatures with a hard skeleton. This definition may thus be used to group organisms very different one from the other: Madreporaria (the true reef builders), Gorgonians, hydrozoans, bryozoans etc. The term coral ought to be used only for the species of the *Corallium* genus (Gorgonacea, the emblematic example being the red

B

C

A

coral of the Mediterranean); it would therefore be more correct to describe the coralline formations as "madreporitic rocks". However, the widespread use of the term "corals" certainly makes the description of these organisms more comprehensible to the public at large and justifies its use in the widest sense of the word.

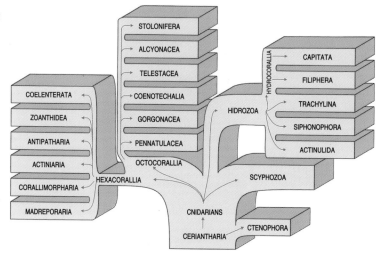

The diagram shows the classification of the Coelenterata group and the Cnidaria phylum. All the organisms making up the coral world (soft corals, fire corals, gorgonians, black corals etc...) belong to the latter. In particular the true reef building corals are only the Hexacorals of the Madreporaria order.

CLASSIFICATION OF CORALS

D

CORAL STRUCTURE

Despite the huge differences in form and dimension between one species and another – visible in the simple examination of a photograph of a tropical reef – corals all share the same basic structure identical also to that of all the Coelenterata, a group of animals belonging to the subkingdom of the metazoans. The Coelenterata owe their name to the presence of a *coelenteron*, a large body cavity, exclusive to these animals; this serves both as a digestive cavity and for the elimination of waste and opens outwards via a single aperture. Another characteristic, essential for the sedentary living habits of these organisms, mobile only at the larva stage, is their radial symmetry: i.e. every animal can be divided according to infinite patterns of symmetry along the radius of an imaginary circle. Besides these common characteristics, the *Cnidaria phylum* – to which corals belong – has a structure called a polyp. This polyp, the primary unit of corals, can be imagined or described as a sort of sac adhering at the base to a rigid substratum and having an aperture facing

E

D - This close up of a madrepore (Montastrea sp.) shows the arrangement of the single polyps, each of which is surrounded and protected by a calcareous theca varying in form from one species to another.

E - The expansion of the polyp, often occurring with very steady rhythms, can considerably change the appearance of a colony of madrepores. The regular external outline of this coral of the Favidae family reflects the radial symmetry of the internal skeleton.

The drawing illustrates the colonial structure of madrepores. These coelenterates consist in a high number of single organisms, the polyps, joined to each other by a common calcareous matrix. Although madrepores are perennially immobile creatures, their polyps can contract (left) and expand (right) thus showing the tentacles and in some cases drastically changing their appearance.

A

A - The polyp structure appears basically as a cylinder of soft tissue communicating with the outside via the mouth. Clearly visible at the top is the crown of tentacles, in multiples of six.

special cases, may consist, in toto or in part, of other "building" organisms belonging to other systematic animal and vegetable groups. Examples of this are the algae reefs of the Bermudas or the reefs of Ferdinando di Noronha and Brazil erected by Rhodophyta (red calcareous algae of the *Neogoniolithon* and *Porolithon* genera) or by vermetid molluscs *(Dendropoma* sp.*)*. Observed closer, the coral polyps have

upwards, surrounded by a variable number of tentacles. The number of these (eight, six or multiples thereof) allows the Anthozoa group to be divided into Octocorallia or Hexacorallia. The Madreporaria belong to this subclass to which a further distinction may be made. A definition, dating from the first half of this century and much used in scientific spheres, considers most corals as hermatypic i.e. organisms capable of building

C

B

D - The corallites of the Favites *genus - common in the Indo-Pacific and present there in twenty or so species - are fused to each other. The walls appear raised and quite regularly circumscribe the mouth of the polyp (centre, open to varying degrees); the tentacles expand mainly at night.*

B - The rigid and compact consistency of the reef building corals is, in many cases, totally hidden by the expanding polyps.

C - The small fish at the centre of the photo is a useful yardstick in calculation of the size of the single polyps, some open, some half-closed.

reefs (from the Greek *erma* = barrier); it defines ahermatypic those organisms, such as Gorgonians, with a horny, flexible skeleton, or soft corals unable to give origin to complex structures capable of resisting the action of the waves.
Over the years, this initial division has been interpreted in various manners and has given rise to numerous distinctions.
An important one associates the presence of symbiont algae or zooxanthellae only with hermatype corals. Recent investigation has indeed confirmed the predominance of hermatype and zooxanthellae species among reef corals although the latter, in

D

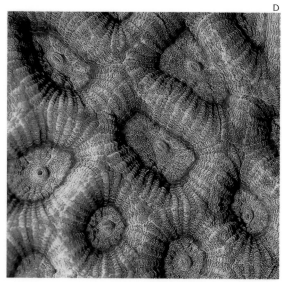

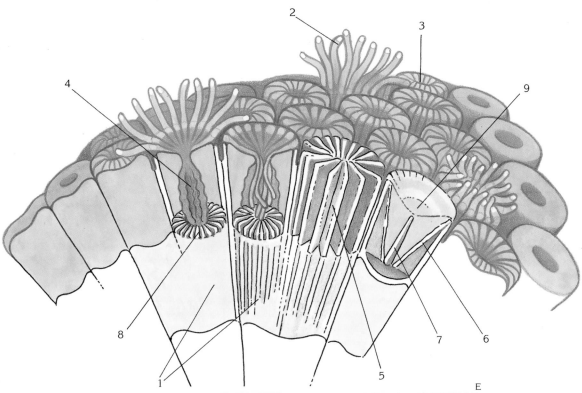

This section of a madrepore reveals the main characteristics of the polyps and how they are arranged in a colony.

1) Calcareous skeleton of dead corallites.
2) Polyps with expanded tentacles.
3) Retracted tentacles.
4) Gastrovascular cavity.
5) Calcareous septa.
6) Theca.
7) Columella.
8) Base plate.
9) Cup or corallite.

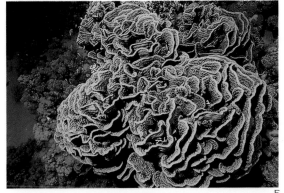

E

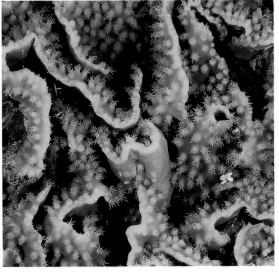

F

E - Easily identified by its intricate convolutions, this Madrepore of the Turbinaria *genus is common in the Indo-Pacific and present there in approximately 15 species. The complex geometry is a result of this species' need to provide the widest possible surface for the symbiont algae associated with the polyps and essential for the survival of the corals.*

F - This close up of the Turbinaria *shows that the small cone-shaped corallites are distinct one from the other and almost exclusively situated on the edges of the convolutions. The tentacles of* the Turbinaria *are, in general, expanded to varying degrees during the day.*

dimensions varying from a few millimetres to approximately one centimetre and may be cylindrical or flat. In section, they appear to have a dual layer of tissue: one external (ectoderm) and one internal (endoderm) separated by a gelatinous layer (mesogloea). Each of these has particular functions (defence, nutrition, limestone synthesis) and forms specific structures. Each polyp communicates with the exterior via the mouth, an oval or elongated fissure entering a short tube (pharynx) and leading to the gastrovascular cavity. This is divided lengthwise by a series of alcoves separated from each other by partitions

A

(mesenteries) converging into the central cavity. The mesenteries play an important role in the digestive processes and participate in the reproductive processes. It is here that the gonads develop. The external wall of the polyp is divided into a base section (calicoblast) and an upper section. The former is responsible for the precipitation of calcium carbonate and is surrounded by a calcareous cup; the latter can swell to hide the skeleton. In the case of solitary or fossil polyps it is particularly easy to observe in detail the skeleton or corallite, typically cylindrical or cup-formed, with a circular or oval section. In this it is possible to distinguish a series of elements for the classification and recognition of the individual species.

The structure of a corallite comprises three principal parts: a base plate, adhering to the substratum, and broad or narrow; a wall or theca, smooth or with streaks or rows of granules (costae); a cavity or cup of varying depths, encompassed by the theca and destined to protect the polyp. Inside the cup other formations can be seen such as the sclerosepta or septa, i.e. vertical partitions arranged radially with a free edge towards the centre of the cup and alternating with the mesenteries. At the centre of the cup usually, though not always, is the columella, consisting in one or more spicules or laminae or in a spongy mass, and the pales, thin axile or laminar structures rising from the cup base and interposed between the edge of the septa and the columella. The septa of a cup are generally of varying dimensions and extend to differing degrees towards the centre. This allows the distinction of 6 larger septa of the first order, 6 of the second order alternating with the former and 12 of the third order set between the previous ones. In line with the septa are the costae, again presenting varying degrees of development.

The septa derive from the secretion of limestone at the base of the polyp which, as a result, is slowly pushed upwards. As the colony grows the corallites

B

leave behind them thick horizontal secretions, called dissepiments, which divide into levels above the colony.

This mechanism gives the vertical growth of coral reefs. The polyps, moreover, are bound to each other by a common skeletal mass, the cenosteum, which may just form a base lamina between the various corallites, as in the case of encrusting species, or it may consitute an arborescent or compact globular mass.

After this general description aimed at clarifying the basic structure of corals, an examination of the various forms may be of use.

The simplest is the cup form, typical mainly in solitary corals – an example is the first corallite of a colony. Some solitary corals are easily distinguished from the rest for their discoidal form similar to the upturned cap of a mushroom.

A, B - The corals of the Fungia *genus are among the most unusual populating coral reefs. Unmistakable for their discoidal form, they are fixed to the substratum only when young. Subsequently, all connections with the sea bottom are lost and they can move autonomously, albeit very slowly. Although they reach some decimetres in size they are single individuals and therefore not colonial. Photograph 4 shows a fungus coral as it expands its tentacles; when completely evaginated they will mask and drastically alter the appearance of the coral. The tentacles are highly efficient in freeing the surface of the Fungidae from the waste and sediment covering it, mainly because these corals often live in sandy areas.*

These are corals of the *Fungia* genus and can be described as a single, large polyp surrounded by its septa; these are fixed to the substratum, when young, by a peduncle, but totally free as adults. They are the only corals capable of moving from their place of settlement. More common are the colonial species, e.g. those of the Favidae family, having different well recognizable corallites, mainly roundish in form or polygonal when very close. These corals are given the name of plocoid corals. In other cases (cerioid corals), the corallites are in such close contact with each other that they present a characteristic fusion of the cup walls (*Goniastrea* genus).

The next stage in the structural evolution of madrepores involves the loss of the walls so that the septa, without interruption, join the centre of a corallite to the next one (thamnasterioid corals) making it difficult to distinguish the single specimens, usually small and irregular. A special case is that of the Agariicidae corals of the *Pachyseris* genus, which form encrusting colonies with the surface marked by concentric reliefs circumscribing lamellate columelle. The cups are indistinct whereas the septa, with finely serrated edges, are very close and arranged in parallel lines. In some corals, the individual corallites and polyps are difficult to distinguish as they are arranged in longitudinal series forming winding furrows and reliefs. In these "brain corals" (*Platygyra, Diploria, Leptoria, Meandrina* genera) the raised parts correspond to the fused walls and the polyps are found at the furrows, where their tiny mouths can also be observed. Despite the validity of this classification, it must be stressed that the variety of colonial corals is so extensive as to sometimes make it difficult to assign a coral to one or other of the above categories. In many cases the form, classifiable in one of four principal morphotypes (ramified, leave-shaped, encrusting and compact) is mainly determined by the way in which new polyps form and the influence of environmental

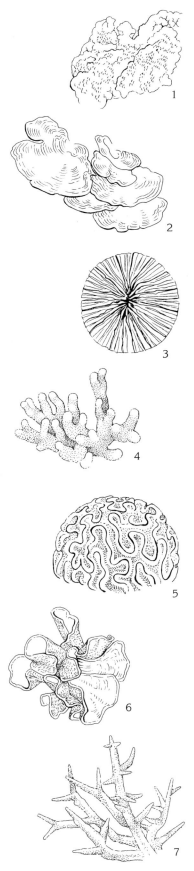

The forms adopted by the various species of Madrepores can be classified within some basic types illustrated below. Each different type is accompanied by the names of some Madrepore genera which colonize as shown.

1 - Encrusting:
Hydnophora, Pseudosiderastrea, Anomastrea.
2 - Lamina-like:
Acropora, Pachyseris, Echinophora, Merulina.
3 - Non sessile:
Fungia, Cycloseris, Polyphyllia, Diaseris, Heliophungia.
4 - Finger-shaped:
Goniopora, Montipora, Dendrophyllia, Tubastrea, Dendrogyra.
5 - Massive:
Porites, Favia, Diploastrea, Goniastrea, Platygyra, Favites, Solenastrea, Isophyllia, Leptoria, Goniopora.
6 - Leaf-like:
Echinophyllia, Pachyseris, Montipora, Echinophora, Turbinaria, Agaricida.
7 - Ramified:
Porites, Seriatopora, Acropora Pocillopora.

factors.

These are particularly obvious in the case of the most adaptable species, thus of high ecological value. A greater hydrodynamism of the water, for instance, favours the development of robust colonies, but in calm waters thinner and more delicate madrepores develop, although the development of the mass forms is not impeded.

This explains why the least exposed parts of a reef appear, on average, richer in variety of form and species than the areas more exposed to the waves or currents. The light intensity, for its close link with symbiont algae, also plays a by no means secondary role and is capable of influencing the form of a colony. A compact, rounded coral in well-illuminated surface waters will, at greater depths where the luminosity is reduced, tend to become flat so as to direct the polyps in a sole direction, thus compensating the reduced action of the sun's rays with a larger surface area.

Similar transformations also occur in ramified corals, such as those belonging to the *Acropora variabilis* species, of which specific ecotypes exist according to the depth, or the Montipora genus, whose colonies, branched in surface waters, tend in deep waters to form tabular structures. Another characteristic of corals, responsible for their "flowered" appearance, is the fact that they have tentacles. These are filiform and not feathered, as occurs for Octocorallia, and their number is 6 or multiples of 6. Anatomically, these can be considered extensions of the polyp around the mouth and they retract inside the cup both following external stimulation or for endogenous rhythms (e.g. the alternation of day and night); they have a defensive function as well as being essential for the capture of food.

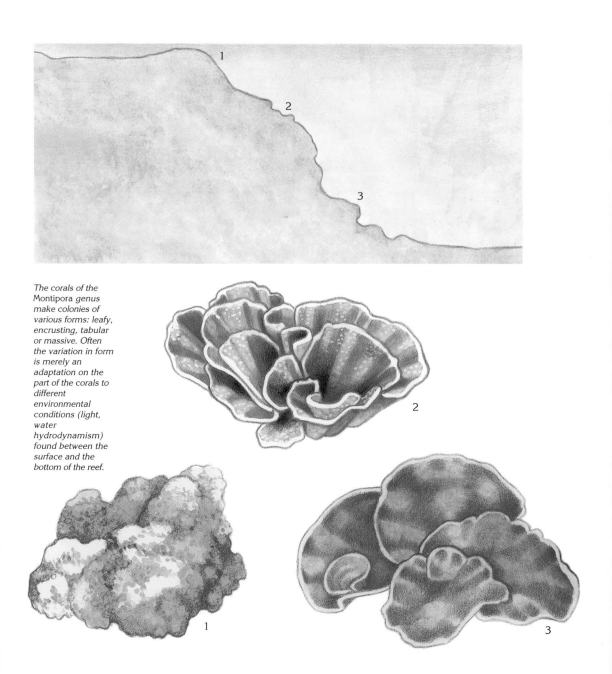

The corals of the Montipora genus make colonies of various forms: leafy, encrusting, tabular or massive. Often the variation in form is merely an adaptation on the part of the corals to different environmental conditions (light, water hydrodynamism) found between the surface and the bottom of the reef.

CORAL REPRODUCTION

Corals reproduce both sexually and asexually. Sexual reproduction is, of course, the fruit of fertilization of eggs by spermatozoa. In light of the most recent studies, the situation is particularly complex as every possible alternative to sexual reproduction is found.
Colonies may be hermaphroditic with the production of eggs and sperm on the same mesenteries

A - The sexual reproduction of corals involves tens and tens of species and thousands of colonies at the same time. On occasions such as these, a diver will witness an extraordinary and fascinating coloured snow shower "falling" onto the surface of the ocean.

*B, C, D - Sexual reproduction in corals involves the simultaneous release of the female and male gametes by all the colonies of madrepores present in an area. This synchronism is controlled by natural phenomena such as the phases of the moon, tides and variations in water temperature. Stimulated by invisible but infallible messengers, the mature gonads release into the water tiny coloured bags containing eggs and spermatozoa which will open on the surface to give birth to a new generation of polyps.
The pictures refer to the mass reproduction that takes place annually, in late spring or early summer, a few nights after the full moon on the Great Barrier Reef and show the moment of the release of numerous bags of gametes from three kinds of corals.
The top picture shows a green honeycomb coral belonging to the Favia genus; at centre, a colony of Favites corals; bottom, a large brain coral Platygyra sinensis, its totally expanded tentacles hiding the regular simmetry of the polyps.*

or on different ones, but always in the same polyp or in different ones of the same colony. In other cases the production of gametes may occur within the same colony, but at different times with the appearance first of the male characteristics and then the female ones or vice versa. There are also corals with distinct sexes, but the number of hermaphroditic species is decidedly higher, especially in the Red Sea and along the Great Barrier Reef of Australia.
Timewise the sexual reproduction of corals may occur monthly, seasonally or annually. Whatever the reproductive cycle of a single species, it is now clear that the gonad maturing processes are influenced by climatic and astronomical factors, the effect of which is aimed at the simultaneous emission of the gametes. This is a particularly important event especially when, as happens in late spring or in early summer along much of the Great Barrier Reef of Australia, more than a hundred species are involved. Actually, the factors involved in the genesis of the phenomenon do not occur simultaneously, but in succession one after the other, the intensity varying from zone to zone. Temperature, for instance, seems to constitute the factor triggering the processes of gametogenesis but its effect in the syncronization of reproduction overlaps that exercised by photoperiodism, i.e. the gradual variation in the duration of day and night.
Many experts, nonetheless, stress the importance of the phases of the moon in the regulation of the

synchronized emission of larvae or gametes which, in most cases, takes place some days after the full moon and always at night; at the same time, limited tide ranges prevent an excessive dispersion of the gametes.
The gonads of the individual polyps mature quickly.
Usually, the female ones start to develop at least six months beforehand, followed approximately two months later by the male ones. They develop slowly during the winter months but accelerate in spring when the surrounding waters warm up rapidly. A month before their emission, the eggs start to become more apparent and acquire a brighter colouring (red, pink, orange or even brown, green or blue) and are visible in transparency or through the mouth, a signal that experts have now learnt to associate with approaching reproduction.
When this involves tens of thousands of corals and extends for hundreds of kilometres as for the Great Australian Barrier Reef, to the eyes of observers it appears as a multicoloured upward snowfall. Obeying a mysterious order and capable of propagation from one madreporitic colony to another, the gametes are expelled through the mouth with varying techniques according to species. Some slowly release the spermatozoa and eggs in separate clusters; others produce a continuous flow of reproductive elements in the form of fine clouds or long chains of granules; others again swell up with water at intervals and forcefully spurt the gametes out. Synchronization is so perfect that corals collected and isolated in an aquarium in the days preceding the event will liberate the gametes in exactly the same period as their similars left on the reef. The dawn following a coral night generally illuminates a sea covered with a coloured mucilaginous film.
Ancient Japanese legends believed this to be the manifestation of the fertility of the female divinities of the ocean. On closer examination, it contains eggs, spermatozoa and

A, B, C - The three photographs (from top to bottom) illustrate the sequence of the expulsion of the gametes in the Goniastrea palauensis species, a brain coral of the Favidae family. Slowly (top photo) the mouth of the polyp dilates to allow the passage of the bag containing the gametes. The pink bag is pushed towards the mouth (centre). The tiny bag containing eggs and spermatozoa is forcefully expulsed and commences its rise to the surface where it will open and release the gametes.

larvae (planulae) developed in the meantime. The encounter between eggs and sperm of the same species, probably guided by chemical factors or by structural differences preventing the cross breeding between different species, must take place as quickly as possible and the subsequent development leads to the formation of a small pear-shaped, ciliated larva of dimensions varying from 0.5 to 2.5 mm. The synchronization of the reproduction, the fact that it occurs mainly at night and the involvement of several species is justified by the need both to increase the probability of encounters between the gametes and to reduce mortality caused by predatory planctivorous fish; this hypothesis is sustained by a number of experts convinced that the relative stability in environmental parameters does not justify such an intense explosion of life, comparable to the increase in planctonic production occurring in temperate waters in spring. As often occurs in the animal world, these beasts of prey are opportunists; they feed on whatever the environment offers in the largest quantities and with the least difficulty.

During coral reproduction many species of fish adopt this rule. Studies conducted on the feeding patterns of various damselfishes have, indeed, shown that within twelve hours of a mass reproduction of madrepores most of the fish examined had a full stomach, proof of the irresistible call exercised on fish by eggs and sperm. Only the enormous quantity of corals involved can guarantee the survival of the number of larvae required for the propagation of the single species. Although external fertilization, a sign of high fertility, seems the most common form of reproduction in Australia and the Red Sea, the most frequent in the Caribbean, Hawaii and central Pacific is internal reproduction – the result of penetration of the sperm into the gastrovascular cavity of the polyp where the eggs adhering to the mesenteries are

D

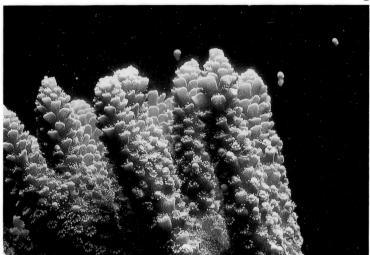

E

fertilized. This type of reproduction gives origin to larvae released into the outside environment only after they have reached a degree of development such to permit ample dispersion. Some experts also suggest that corals with small polyps produce fewer eggs than those with large polyps, and that fertilization occurs internally in the former and externally in the latter. A typical example of a species with internal fertilization is the *Pocillopora damicornis*, common all over the Pacific; at the moment of their release, its planulae already contain zooxanthellae together with a fair quantity of reserve fats which also have the advantage of favouring floating. Besides the intrinsic ability of all the larvae to nourish themselves

D, E - All the polyps in a colony (the bottom photo shows a detail of Acropora secale *during the first phase of reproduction) are involved in the reproductive event and release the coloured sacs containing the gametes almost simultaneously or in rapid succession. Above it is possible to observe a detail of the tips of* Acropora tenuis *with the sacs containing eggs and spermatozoa just freed and soon to float on the surface.*

A

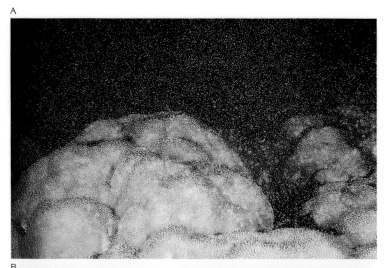

B

A - A large colony of cushion madrepores enveloped in a cloud of gametes during spawning, the term generally used to describe the massive emission of eggs and spermatozoa by an organism in a specific period of time.

B - Some species of madrepores, such as this Fungia fungites *are not hermaphrodites like other corals. In this case there are females and males, such as that photographed emitting a small cloud of sperm destined to fertilize the eggs released by females of the same species.*

occurred, this shows how long these organisms remain alive. The planulae coming from external fertilization of the gametes are, in contrast, devoid of zooxanthellae although they may absorb them from the surrounding environment in the initial stages of growth. The duration of the planctonic phase of a larva is also considered a factor capable of determining the composition in species of a reef. Those of the eastern Pacific in particular consist mainly in species with larvae having a widespread dispersion. An abundance of endemic species is, instead, almost always linked to larvae having a very brief planctonic phase. Studies conducted on madrepores belonging to the *Favia* and *Pocillopora* genera reveal that initially the larvae are positively influenced by light. This enables them to remain in the surface strata of the water and, thus, to be dispersed more easily by waves and currents, as described above. The planctonic life phase involves however great danger for the planulae, and only a limited number remain vital until the moment of settlement. This is preceded by physiological changes, the most obvious manifestation being the appearance of a negative phototropism which induces the planulae to direct themselves towards the sea bottom in search of a suitable substratum. The choice of the place in which to settle is a critical moment in the life of a coral larva although some species such as *Seriatopora hystrix* and *Pocillopora damicornis* can leave the place originally chosen should this prove unsuitable. Among the factors influencing the adhesion of the planulae to the substrata are the degree of illumination on the sea bottom and its unevenness. Equally important, but capable of interfering mainly on the recruitment of new colonies, is the action exercised by herbivorous organisms (gasteropods and sea-urchins), which in passing may eliminate newly settled larvae, and sedimentation which may

independently during the planctonic life phase, these planulae, called teleplanic, remain vital for over a hundred days, long enough to be dispersed over wide areas. At least four species of corals found in the Bermudas seem to originate in the Bahamas, 1,700 kilometres away, thanks to the larvae carried from one to the other end of the Caribbean by the Gulf Stream. Even more extraordinary is the report of floating fragments of pumice-stone, originated during a volcanic eruption in the Revillagigedo Islands off Mexico and found in the Marshall Islands encrusted with small colonies of corals. It was calculated that the pumice-stones had travelled over 8,700 kilometers in approximately 560 days and, although the experts were not able to establish where the settlements suffocate them. Other factors may intervene in the choice of a suitable substratum, e.g. the presence of colonies of the same species, as already seen in other sessile invertebrates having planctonic larvae (e.g. in cirripede crustaceans of the *Balanus* genus, in oysters or ascidians). Because of their simple structure corals are capable of reproducing asexually, also within the hermaphroditic species; examples are not lacking especially in the eastern Pacific, parts of the Hawaiian islands, in southern Australia and probably also in the Bermudas. Asexual reproduction by fragmentation is important for many species and especially for those which, because of their over intense or prolonged development and for the shortage of new generations, are close to their physiological limits. The same occurs in areas where preying on the young is very intense. Reproduction by fragmentation allows a more rapid propagation of the populations and increases the probabilities of survival of the new colonies thanks to their dimensions and the greater ability to resist sedimentation. In regions where the conditions are generally optimum, growth by fragmentation may be dominant wherever there is a predominance of flat, sandy sea bottoms whereas walls with a steeper slope, in the case of madreporitic species, depend on the settlement of larvae.

C

D

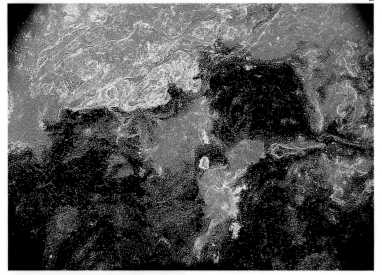

E

C - The mass of gametes released at the same time by thousands and thousands of madrepores turns the surface of the water into a sort of gelatinous mixture that traps the most varied objects.

D, E - The great "snowfall" covers vast expanses of sea with a multi-coloured mixture of eggs, spermatozoa and larvae; some peoples of the Indo-Pacific considered this a manifestation of the fertility of the sea.

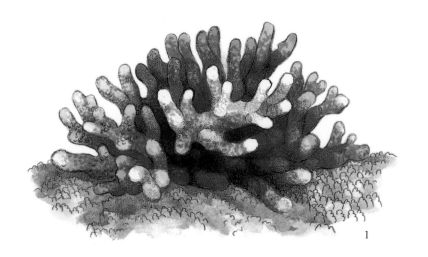

1

Corals sometimes also reproduce by fragmentation. This occurs in particular in those populations of madrepores close to their physiological limits or that develop in areas where preying on the young is very intense. In these cases a part of a coral broken away from the main colony (1) and carried by the waves during a storm can survive and slowly fix itself to the substratum (2); it will start to grow again giving rise to a new independent colony (3).

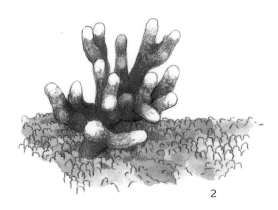

2

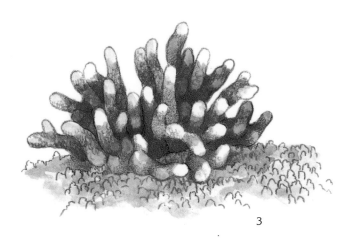

3

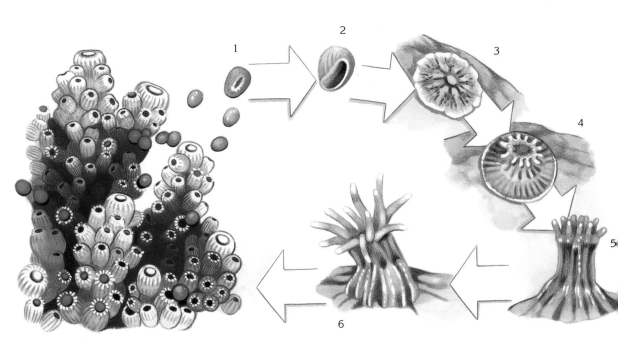

The drawing illustrates in detail the main phases of the life cycle of a madrepore.
1) During the reproduction period the sexually mature colonies release their gametes.
2) The union between eggs and spermatozoa leads to the formation of a small ciliate larva called planula; this is capable of surviving for a period in the water leading a planktonic life at the mercy of the currents.
3) At the moment of metamorphosis the larva moves close to the sea bed adhering to it in a sort of flat disc with the mouth turned upwards.
4) Immediately the base cells of the new polyp start to secrete an initial layer of calcareous matter firmly fixing the polyp to the substratum.
5) Slowly the polyp takes shape and creates the corallite, the rigid part shaped like a cup serving to protect it.
6) The definitive growth of the first corallite represents the beginning of the gradual development which will lead to the formation of a new colony.

At the end of the larval life phase, the coral planula fixes itself to the substratum and undergoes certain modifications.

Initially it secretes a thin layer of mucus and then changes form to become flat, although the mouth remains directed upwards. Curiously, at this stage some species are capable of performing a reverse metamorphosis if the conditions of the sea bottom are not ideal and, as a result, return to planctonic life and the search for a better site.

The lower part of the larva, now a disc, starts immediately to secrete calcareous material from the ectodermic base cells.

These produce filaments of a chitinous nature among which rigid crystals formed by a solution over-saturated with calcium ions are deposited. These primary crystals bond together to form crystalline fibres of aragonite, a special form of calcareous material, and make up the structural parts of the corallites described above: theca, ribs, septa etc. Temperature has a great influence on the physiological reactions leading to the deposit of calcareous material. Synthesis of this material is slow at temperatures of less than 15°C, but increases steadily between 15° and 28°C. (optimum 25-27°C), slowing down again beyond 30°C. The relation between synthesis and temperature effectively explains the limits of the geographical distribution of the corals described in the previous chapter, although some studies have revealed the existence of specific adaptations in the populations of each species. The Pocillopora damicornis, for instance, in the Hawaiis presents an optimum growth at a temperature of 27°C, whereas on the atoll of Eniwetok (Marshall Islands) it seems to have two optimum temperatures: 27° and 31°C.

The ordered and regular apposition of aragonite crystals leads in the end to the construction of the first corallite, a solitary existence destined to last approximately one week. Very soon an enlargement

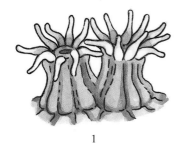

1

The arrangement of the polyps (1) depends on the growth processes of the colony, shown here in a longitudinal section (above series) and cross section made in correspondence of the oral disc (bottom series).

With the so-called intratentacular growth process a polyp (2) undergoes a progressive strangling at the centre of the oral disc; this in the end forms an increasingly accentuated figure of eight (3).

The final phase (4) coincides with the formation of two separate polyps, side by side and joined by the calcareous matrix and a thin layer of tissue.

2

3

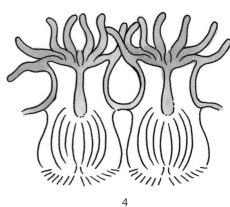

4

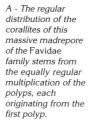

A - The regular distribution of the corallites of this massive madrepore of the Favidae family stems from the equally regular multiplication of the polyps, each originating from the first polyp.

A

1a

B

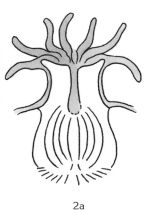

2a

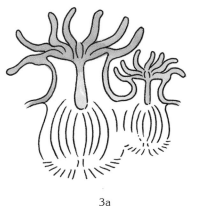

3a

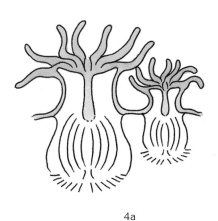

4a

The presence of polyps side by side but of different sizes (1a) is often due to an extratentacular process of colony growth. By this mechanism, illustrated both in longitudinal (above series) and cross section made in correspondence of the oral disc (bottom series), from a *"mother" polyp (2a) there is an evagination of the outer wall (3a); this gradually becomes more defined with the formation of the tentacles and a mouth. In the end (4a) the junction between the two polyps is broken and the new one starts to secrete its own corallite.*

producing a small bud will appear. This is the process by which a colony of madrepores is formed and occurs in two principal manners. The first is called intratentacular and resembles a process of cellular fission.
The oral disc of the "mother" polyp folds inwards until it resembles an 8, increasingly accentuated until two distinct mouths appear, all the organs (tentacles, mesenteries etc.) and structures (theca, costae) are doubled and two polyps of the

same dimensions are formed.
A true and proper gemmation is the other mechanism by which a coral multiplies. This process is called extratentacular and is manifested with an evagination of the external wall of the mother polyp; this increases progressively until a small mouth is formed, then a circle of tentacles and, in the end, a new, smaller, polyp which starts to secrete its own casing. Whatever the method of formation of the new polyps, the process is

A

B

C

D

A, B, C, D - Madrepores, the reef builders, come in the widest variety of shapes, greatly differing from one species to another or different within the same species depending on the habitat in which the colony is growing. From top to bottom the pictures show the main type of coral shapes: massive, ramified, cushion and leafy.

repeated with growing speed, almost a chain reaction, to produce a colony of thousands upon thousands of identical polyps, all descending from the first corallite and all bound together by a common calcareous matrix in densities which may vary from a few polyps to several dozen per square centimetre. Other larvae, identical or of other species, may settle alongside or in the vicinity and over thousands of years grow in the same way to form a reef. Of course the nature and growth of the latter will depend on all the factors described in the preceding pages. The final result will be the birth of an extraordinary spring of life destined to grow by mechanisms related by cause and effect, which can be thus resumed: increase in productivity and biomass, increase in the colonized surface, increase in the number of ecological niches, increase in the number of species.

Although the metabolic processes leading to the synthesis of calcareous material are the same for all madrepores, the speed with which the skeletons of the colonies are constructed is highly variable. Compact corals may grow less than 1 centimetre per year whereas some Acroporas can, in particularly favourable conditions, record increases of 20 centimetres per year. What mechanisms lead to the synthesis of calcareous material? The calcium required for the construction of the skeletons is drawn directly from the sea water in ionic form (Ca^{++}), but in order to become solid calcium carbonate ($Ca(HCO_3)_2$) it must combine with bicarbonate ions (HCO_{-3}) derived from the separation of carbonic acid (H_2CO_3).

Unfortunately the reaction is not very effective and is unstable as the solid substance tends to dissolve as soon as it forms. If the calcium carbonate is to be formed in sufficient quantities for the construction of a reef, it is essential that carbonic acid coming from the union of carbon dioxide and water is eliminated as quickly as possible; in corals this occurs thanks to the presence of zooxanthellae.

A colony grows in size thanks to the constant formation of new polyps; their skeletons are destined, at their death, to become the base for the growth of other polyps. The size and form of each colony varies from one species to another but, generally speaking, corals can be divided into two main categories: massive corals, e.g. Favidae and brain corals (drawing no.1) and ramified corals, e.g. Acroporidae and Pocilloporidae (drawing no.2).

A longitudinal section of madrepore, appropriately treated, allows experts to calculate the age of the colony and the annual growth, the latter depending both on the seasons and on the physiological conditions of the coral.

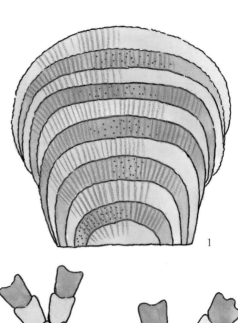

1

E

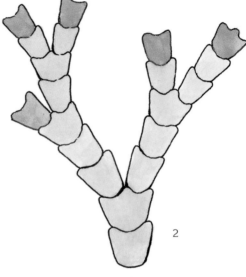

2

F

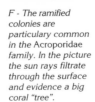

E - Every coral species settles on a reef and grows where environmental conditions are most favourable.
As occurs in the forest, corals on a reef influence each other and compete for space.

F - The ramified colonies are particulary common in the Acroporidae family. In the picture the sun rays filtrate through the surface and evidence a big coral "tree".

G - A specimen of finger-form or columnar madrepore has grown on the reef just a few metres under the surface.

G

59

Precious and vital: zooxanthellae

The browny-green or bluey-green colouring characterizing most polyps is to be attributed to the presence of zooxanthellae in their tissue. These are unicellular algae, or to be more precise dinoflagellates of the *Symbiodinium adriaticum* species living inside the endodermal cells of the coral. The association between these algae and corals is very close. It is actually an endosymbiosis of a mutual nature from which both organisms benefit. The zooxanthellae supply the polyp with energy in the form of products obtained by photosynthesis including sugars, amino acids and glycerol, plus small quantities of vitaminic and hormonal substances.
The algae also enrich the surrounding environment with oxygen and remove potentially toxic compounds such as carbon dioxide, phosphorous and nitrogen. These products come mainly from the coral metabolism and are its principal contribution to the symbiosis as well as that of providing the algae with a fairly stable environment safe from predators. Of particular importance is the role played by carbon dioxide. This gas, excreted by all organisms as a final product of respiration, tends to unite with water to form carbonic acid, a compound which, for its nature, tends to dissolve the calcium carbonate skeleton of the coral and slow down synthesis.
The process of photosynthesis, of which carbon dioxide and water are the starting products, allows the zooxanthellae to continuously remove the carbon dioxide, thus lowering the acidity of the environment and favouring, as a result, the reactions leading to the formation of the skeleton as described previously.
This explains why hermatypic corals are also zooxanthellate. The fast growth of corals is therefore due exclusively to the symbiont algae hosted in considerable quantities in the coral tissues. It has been calculated that

A

B

every square centimetre of coral tissue contains roughly a million algae, and these are continuously being renewed to maintain the concentration stable. If corals are deprived of their zooxanthellae, the formation of the skeleton is reduced and almost disappears. This is one of the major threats to the survival of these organisms, as has already occurred following environmental changes (pollution from toxic substances, temperature rise) which, in some coral areas (e.g. in the Bermudas in 1987 and 1988), have caused first the death of the zooxanthellae and subsequently that of the madrepores, manifested in the total whitening of long stretches of

A, B - The coloured tissues of the Tridacna contain thousands of microscopic symbiont algae. The association is identical to that found in corals between polyps and zooxanthellae. In the Tridacna the algae are concentrated mainly around the light parts of the covering. These are like small sheets of transparent glass and allow the passage of the sun's rays - essential for the survival of the zooxanthellae.

C - The browny green colouring distinguishing many Madrepore polyps is usually produced by the presence of symbiont algae. These are called zooxanthellae and belong to the Symbiodinium adriaticum *species*.

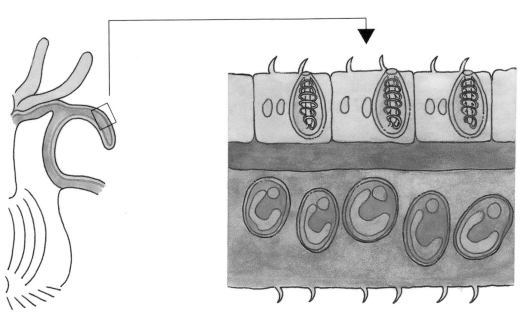

The section diagram illustrates the arrangement of the main coral polyp tissues.
1 Salmon pink = the ectoderm.
2 Red = the intermediary stratum or mesogloea.
3 Green = the endoderm.

The diagram imagines a large magnification of a section of polyp tentacle (the colours of the tissues are the same as in the previous drawing). The spiral structure represents the stinging filaments of the nematocysts used by the polyps for defence and capture.
The roundish formations in the green layer are the zooxanthellae.

These photsynthetic cells are not found in the tentacles alone but may also appear in the deeper parts of the polyp, where food is digested. Despite the location they are equally influenced by the light because coral tissue is thin and fairly transparent.

rocks. The presence of the zooxanthellae also explains why the best developed corals are found in the first 20-30 metres below the surface and how the limit for their growth is to be placed, and only in exceptional cases, at a depth of approximately 90 metres The essential requirement for the performance of the metabolic functions of the zooxanthellae and coral life is light. Studies conducted on the Great Barrier Reef, where for experimental purposes some colonies or corals were screened, showed that when deprived of light they died within six months.
The relationships between corals and symbiont algae are far more

A

A - As seen in this photograph, colonies of building corals tend to direct their growth so as to be always exposed to the light. Exactly as occurs in a forest - a habitat having many affinities with coral reefs - every species has evolved so as to best exploit the natural resources available required for growth and survival.

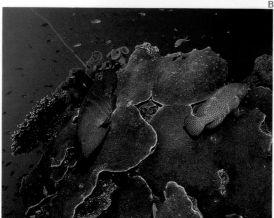

B

B - Similar to encrusting algae, these leafy agaricid corals adhere to the substratum arranging their corallites in concentric and horizontal rows. This allows the colony to expose to the sunlight the largest possible number of zooxanthellae; these are essential for the growth of the corals

*and for calcareous synthesis. Very often colonies of the same species vary in form, from massive to leafy, as the depth increases.
The distance from the surface directly influences the transmission of the luminous waves in the water, reducing energy and forcing the corals to adapt accordingly.*

complex than hitherto described. The use of radioactive tracers has revealed that ramified colonies have systems of circulation and transportation by which the substances produced by the algae can be concentrated and used above all at the tip of the branches, where growth is most intense.
The relationship between vegetable and animal is so close that, if the algae are experimentally cultivated in the absence of corals, their efficiency in the production of the organic substances used by the polyps is reduced by 30%-40% to less than 10%. Corals, in turn, especially those growing close to the surface or subject to periodical emersion during low tide, secrete special substances which act as a filter against the harmful UV rays which could destroy their zooxanthellae. The connection

between light and coral growth is also confirmed in calcium carbonate deposition cycles. Examination of the sections of coral colonies has revealed that the rhythms of the synthesis of calcareous material are not only annual, but daily; it is possible to calculate the age of a single colony using a technique similar to that of counting the rings on a tree trunk. A detailed study conducted over 24 hours of the microscopic events in the points where coral growth is most active has shown that during the day calcification is 2-3 times more rapid than at night and that the alternation of light/darkness also influences the type of calcium carbonate crystals produced by the tissues of the polyp; there is an alternation between fusiform ones, deposited at night, and needle-shaped ones formed during the

C

day. The annual rhythms can be highlighted using X ray techniques, with UV sensitive colourings or with sophisticated gamma ray densitometry investigation.
The growth bands have allowed evaluation of the speed of growth of different species or of the same species in different locations. They have also permitted the study of fossil corals and thus revealed that approximately 370 million years ago a year lasted almost 400 days, confirming the astronomical theories by which the speed of the earth's rotation had gradually slowed down.

D

E

C - The association between corals and gorgonians enables us to assess the importance of certain environmental factors (currents for the gorgonians, light for the corals) essential in the survival of these organisms.

D - The delicate fluorescent colours of these polyps are produced by the high concentration of zooxanthellae; in some cases these may reach the incredible number of a million cells per cubic centimetre of coral tissue.

E, F - Polyps, with their delicate almost impalpable shape, consist in an outer ectoderm, the mesogloea, intermediary layer and the endoderm.

F

A universe of predators

Corals turn to various methods and sources to satisfy their nutritional requirements. It is known that they can absorb organic and inorganic substances from the outside environment, but it is still not certain how important, in terms of energy yield, this contribution may be. They can, in part, use their own zooxanthellae, a hypothesis borne out by the almost total absence of free zooxanthellae in corals. The most important source of nourishment for the majority of the species is, nonetheless, plankton even though the bigger corals can also capture larger

A

Longitudinal section of a coral polyp tentacle.

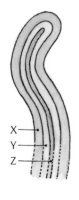

Tentacles are hollow structures consisting in an external ectoderm (x) and an internal endoderm (z) separated by a gelatinous layer called mesogloea (y).

Enlarged section of a polyp.

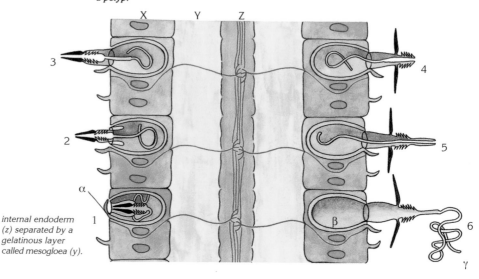

organisms, dead or weakened beyond capability of defence. Many corals are active and efficient predators capable of capturing with their tentacles any prey hovering around them or carried by the currents. Their tentacles have stinging cells to capture and kill the prey. These are globular cells (cnidoblasts) and enclose a long and very thin filament (nematocyst) wound in a spiral. When an animal comes in contact with one of these cells, the latter opens immediately violently

expelling the nematocysts which penetrate the body of the victim, injecting it with a toxic secretion via the long hollow filament. Although the first attack is determined by the contact between the prey and the stinging cell, it now seems certain that the discharge of the subsequent nematocysts, essential for the sure capture of the prey, is caused by chemical stimulus from the prey itself. Coral polyps are sensitive to the organic substances (amino acid sugars) contained in the intracellular liquids of their

These are hollow structures: from the outside inwards are the ectoderm (x) and endoderm (z) separated by a gelatinous mass called mesogloea (y). An enlarged section of the tentacle showing the order of the tissues (ectoderm, mesogloea, endoderm) and the stinging cells or cnidoblasts (ß). Shown clockwise (from 1 to 6) is the sequence leading to the liberation of the stinging filament or

nematocysts ( ) connected. When a cnidoblast comes into contact with a foreign body which stimulates the sensitive cnidocil ( ) this opens immediately (2) and the stinging filament, normally wound in a spiral, is violently projected outwards (3-4-5) by the pressure created inside the cnidoblast. At the end of the sequence the whole filament appears evaginated.

potential prey.

A mixture of homogenized plankton and water in concentrations of 10 mg/l is capable of stimulating a clear response in corals which open their mouths and move their tentacles more intensely in search of the food. Despite this, the hunting by corals is practically blind and their success depends on the concentration of prey in the water. Since this tends to increase at night when the zooplankton rise towards the surface, coral polyps will tend to appear expanded during the night and sometimes drastically modify the appearance of the colonies, seemingly lined with thousands of tentacles in motion. Both the tentacles and the cnidoblasts are covered with a sticky mucus. This can retain particles of organic detritus or bacteria then conveyed towards the mouth either directly by the tentacles or by rows of microscopic vibratile cilia tidily arranged on their surface.

The cilia also serve to eliminate any sediment from the surface of the tentacles or to drive away residue food and waste products expelled from the mouth.

For this purpose they can invert the direction of vibration as need be. This special ability of corals contrasts, however, with the relative lack of plankton along coral reefs and their high productivity depends mainly on the rapid recycling of food between corals and algae, on favourable environmental conditions and on the abundance of ecological niches. Recent research has shown that corals can use other food resources to integrate those captured independently. They can use dissolved substances, amino acids and vitamins absorbing them directly through their tissues. Laboratory experimentation has shown that corals manage to live in sea water devoid of plankton if there is sufficient illumination and a presence of organic substances. Their growth is obviously slower, but the experiment was successful in showing the high degree of self-sufficiency of these organisms.

B

C

A - Despite their inoffensive appearance corals are capable of capturing species relatively large in size compared with their polyps.

a

b

c

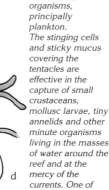

d

B - The stinging capacity of the defensive cells of corals and the harpoon effect of the nematocysts can paralyze and kill many organisms; these are then slowly swallowed by the polyp.

C - The feeding habits of corals hover between those of a typical carnivorous predator and those of a herbivore thanks to the presence of the zooxanthellae, corals benefiting from the excess photosynthetic output of these symbionts.

Corals are predatory organisms capable of capturing various organisms, principally plankton.
The stinging cells and sticky mucus covering the tentacles are effective in the capture of small crustaceans, mollusc larvae, tiny annelids and other minute organisms living in the masses of water around the reef and at the mercy of the currents. One of these organisms coming into contact with one or more tentacles (a) remains trapped (b). Subsequently, the tentacles and the invisible vibratory cilia covering them drive the prey towards the mouth (c) and from here they are conducted into the gastrovascular cavity for digestion (d).

LIFE ON A REEF

A

B

C

A - The extraordinary variety of colours and life forms captivate the increasing number of divers along coral reefs and hide complex relationships between one organism and another. Distracted by the beauty of the sea bed, it is nearly always difficult for the diver to grasp that before his very eyes life and death, builders and destroyers, allies and enemies are all caught up in the battle for survival.

B - Often invisible, worms are practically omnipresent in coral reefs, reaching inconceivable densities. A block of dead coral weighing just 3 kg examined by a team of experts on the Great Barrier Reef contained more than 1300 worms belonging to about a hundred different species. Common and conspicuous representatives of this hidden universe are the Christmas Tree worms (Spirobranchus giganteus); defended by the corals on which they settle, only the coloured tentacles used for breathing and feeding protrude.

C - Gorgonians, usually easily recognized by their fan shape, on close examination prove a veritable mini microcosm. Their skeletons are attacked by encrusting organisms such as Alcyonacea and sponges and although their appearance is not altered, contrasting patches of colour are created. In other cases the Gorgonians become an excellent prop for organisms such as sea lilies which need to extend their feathery arms well out into the water to feed.

The fascinating multicoloured scenario of coral reefs conceals a close-knit and complex series of relationships between predators and prey; both are engaged in the eternal battle for existence and, as has effectively been claimed by some experts the finishing line of this race for survival is always farther away.

Numerous biological and comportmental factors are involved (reproduction, defence, competition etc.) and act simultaneously to govern the distribution and sequence of population. This is especially true for bottom or benthic ones and in the conquest of space and resources needed for growth. Preying, often masked and unrecognizable, is one of the principal mechanisms preventing a few organisms from monopolizing a reef and the colonization of the surfaces by encrusting organisms such as corals, algae, sponges, worms, ascidians and molluscs.

Together, despite the constant and rapid succession of the subjects, these will in time create a stable community. One of the best examples of "hidden" competition occurs in corals.

The distribution of Madrepore colonies in a reef is not influenced by physical factors alone, as outlined in the previous chapters, but also by biological factors depending on the corals themselves as population density represents the first limitation to their growth.

A comparison of the various species would lead to the conclusion that those with a rapid growth could easily prevail over the others and thus produce rocks consisting only of *Acropora* and similar species. In actual fact it is not so; a scale exists and, strangely, the small, slow-growing species predominate over the faster growing and more conspicuous ones.

Rapid growth, although useful, is thus only one of the means used by corals to gain the space required. In a far more effective manner, coral polyps can use their long extending filaments, normally

D - The photo looking down on these two colonies of tabular colonies clearly shows the point of contact between the two structures. No one knows what will happen at this stage: which of the corals will win or whether they will both survive, simply expanding in opposite directions.

E - The co-existence of two or more coral colonies is not always resolved with a peaceful sharing of the space. Governed by strict laws regulating the possibilities of settlement during the larval phase and their subseqent expansion, corals compete to grow using chemical arms and a faster or slower growth - they will, however, work relentlessly to undermine the enemy.

serving for extragastric digestion, as weapons against nearby corals and other organisms.

Having cells capable of secreting powerful enzymes as well as stinging cnidoblasts, the most aggressive corals use these to eliminate their neighbours, digesting them or inhibiting their growth.

The strength of the digestive enzymes differs from one species to another and this difference creates a social hierarchy between the Madrepores. For this reason the distribution of corals on a reef is very probably the result of silent battles between different species as, too, between colonies of the same species. Sometimes there is an alternation of aggressive and non-aggressive forms within a single species.

This seems linked to time factors and governed by environmental and physiological factors.

The madrepore colonies would thus appear capable of recognizing subtle differences between conspecific subjects with physiological processes similar to the reactions of rejection observed in transplant patients.

A typical example is *Stylophora pistillata* with its purple colonies and yellow subordinate ones.

The stinging cells of the dominant and more aggressive colonies induce necrosis of the polyps of nearby colonies, subsequently attacked and covered with algae,

bacteria and other disintegrating microorganisms. In other cases, the growth of the subordinate colony is impeded by a massive proliferation of its rival which erects a sort of barrier between the two Madrepores.

In other cases again, the more aggressive colony manages to absorb the closest parts of its adversary until total fusion is achieved.

Chemical and physical defence mechanisms are also used against predators by other Anthozoans such as Gorgonians which, unlike the stinging anenomes, to the eyes of the diver appear totally harmless.

F - The meeting of two colonies may trigger mechanisms of competition similar to phenomena of rejection in humans after transplants. The tip of the ramified coral (left) seems almost to dissolve and disintegrate on contact with the edge of the other colony. Following the death of the polyps, the Madrepore skeleton loses all powers of defence and is soon attacked by the algae, sponges and other encrusting organisms which will accelerate its destruction.

They defend themselves from predators, in this case mainly gastropod molluscs e.g. those of the *Ciphoma* genus typical of the Caribbean or fish (*Thalassoma sp.*), by secreting special toxic or repellent substances, principally terpenes, fatty acids and nitrogenous compounds, which make their tissues unpleasant. Sclerites are also effective deterrents: these characteristic calcareous formations strengthen the skeletons of Gorgonians and

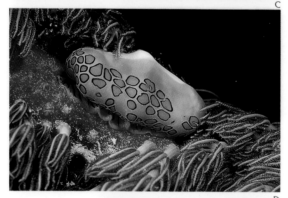

soft corals, again harmless in appearance but with specific protection systems.

The Gorgonians almost seem to have a precise defence strategy as both the sclerites and the repellent substances are concentrated in the younger, weaker and more vulnerable tips. Chemical defences are also adopted by simple invertebrates such as sponges, evolved Ascidiacea, some of which can even secrete compounds with a corrosive action comparable to that of a concentrated acid, and many nudibranchs, in particular those feeding on hydropolyps and sponges. The Ascidiacea manage to conserve intact the stinging cells on the tentacles of their prey and transfer them undamaged to the fluctuating papillae of their body, thus transformed into a stinging morsel discouraging all attempts at assault. Nudibranchs feed on sponges and use the calcareous or siliceous spicules contained in the Porifera to make their tissues rough and hard. Unfortunately, not even these solutions are free from imperfections. For the molluscs mentioned similar defences are to no avail against carnivorous nudibranchs.

A - Sponges (Callyspongia plicifera) and Gorgonians are a common sight on the Caribbean reefs where these organisms abound, the reverse being true for the reefs of the Indo-Pacific The different eating habits allow both species to grow close to each other and in most cases this occurs where regular currents rich in plankton prevail.

B - The extraordinary fans of the giant Gorgonians of the Red Sea (Subergorgia hicksoni) successfully withstand the action of all predatory organisms with their fairly rapid growth and perhaps, as occurs in other Gorgonians, by means of pointed spicules.

C - The gastropod molluscs, called Flamingo's tongue (Ciphoma gibbosum), after the characteristic patches on the porcelain-like shell, feed on the Gorgonian polyps. These manage however to protect their most tender parts by secreting toxic and repellent substances, mainly belonging to the category of oxygenated sesquiterpenes and by increasing the number of spicules in the tissues covering the skeleton.

D - The position adopted by Gorgonians in the water is influenced by the direction of the prevailing currents. By growing perpendicular to these, the Gorgonians' polyps have a constant supply of clean water, oxygen and nourishment. For this reason, many sessile organisms, such as ascidians and bivalve molluscs e.g. Lopha cristagalli with its zig zag valves covered with a red sponge, settle on the fans.

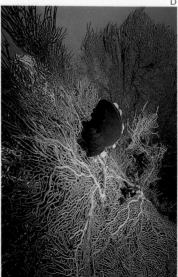

of many other invertebrates including the large clams depend, are the first stage in every food pyramid and on reefs provide the principal source of nourishment for the plentiful herbivorous fish as too molluscs and echinoderms.

The most typical plant-eating fish are burners (surgeonfish, Pomacentridae, butterflyfish, triggerfish, rabbit fish, pufferfish) with sharp teeth capable of cutting algae to pieces and scraper fish (various species of blenny and goby) which, instead, remove the algal covering on the substratum with teeth like rasps. Other species also manage to exploit the most concealed algae or those bound to the corals. This is the case of parrotfish whose teeth are fused together to form four plates (two lower and two upper). These make a hard beak capable of biting

A

The life of the organisms living on a coral reef depends on the respect of mutual relationships involving the selection and defence of the habitat, the choice of a partner and on reproduction. The crucial factor for every species remains the need to eat and not be eaten. This leads to countless adaptations and types of feeding behaviour that make the trophic systems of the reef particularly complex. The diagram illustrates the principal relationships between producers and consumers.
The algae (1) present on the reef, including those associated with the corals, nourish rich populations of herbivorous fish such as surgeonfish and various Labridae, Blennidae and Gobiidae (2). The detritus on the sea bottom (3) and the remains of dead organisms constitute a primary source of food for the invertebrates (4) and for fish such as Mugilidae (5) or goat fish (6) which supplement this diet abundantly with benthic organisms. These are also captured by the large invertebrates such as octopus (7), a large number of fish such as butterflyfish (8), grunters (9) and small Serranidae such as Anthias (10). The small

fish, primary or sometimes secondary consumers, are attacked by the larger species on the reef, including the Lutjanidae or snappers (11) and the groupers (12) which represent the vanguard of the fish at the top of the coral reef food pyramid such as sharks (13), barracudas (14) giant grouper (15) and Carangids (16). Another food chain with many of its links tied up with those of the categories hitherto described starts with phytoplankton or vegetable plankton (17), the basic nourishment of zooplankton (18) responsible for the survival of various species of fish, among which many damselfish (19) and clupeids (20) or other small shoal fish. Characteristic of the coral reef is the food chain based on corals (21). These invertebrates could almost be considered half carnivore and half herbivore because their diet includes both plankton and their symbiont algae (zooxanthellae) and are actively hunted by many butterflyfish (8), by parrot fish (22), porcupine fish (23) and even Monacanthidae (24). These can, in turn, become prey to the large predators situated at the top of the chain.

A - The large rays with their discoidal, flattened body such as the well known blue spotted lagoon ray (Taeniura lymma), have well adapted to life on the sea bottom. They not only rest here or hide covering themselves with sediment, they also find nourishment using rapid strokes of the fins to uncover crustaceans, molluscs and fish living buried in the sea floor.

B - Angelfish, represented here by the emperor angelfish Pomacanthus imperator, have a small mouth with brushlike teeth and feed mainly on sponges encrusted with algae, although this special diet is supplemented with

other invertebrates and vegetables.
The Pomacanthidae family also includes almost exclusively herbivorous species and others feeding on planktonic organisms and small benthic invertebrates such as bryozoa and polychaeta and on algae.

B

deeply into the coral surface. The mass swallowed is then minced by special pharyngeal teeth similar to plates and, when practically reduced to dust, it is expelled from the anus in the form of characteristic clouds. It has been calculated that a population of parrotfish can every year produce up to a ton of coral sand per hectare, a remarkable quantity although it seems to be far less than the sediments created individually by sea urchins, equally specialized herbivores. The traces of the passage of parrotfish are clearly visible on corals and their presence can be perceived from a distance as the noise of the beaks on the Madrepores is so clear that an attentive ear can make out the size of the fish busy feeding.

The adults produce a duller, more prolonged sound than the rapid, sharp one of the young.

The Pomacentridae are perhaps more specialized herbivores and establish special nutritional bonds with their territory. They favour the growth of an algal covering impeding the expansion of the

encrusting algae and corals essential for the reef structure, which at that point will be more markedly subject to separation. Fish also influence other aspects of reef life such as nitrogen fixation or the populations of minor animals by leaving a base layer of red algae which serves as a refuge for the younger forms of many invertebrates, not by chance more abundant in these "private gardens" than elsewhere.

To obtain these results the Pomacentridae systematically destroy the polyps of the corals present on their territory and then defend it fiercely against all other fish with similar feeding habits. Although algae may for their simplicity appear as preordained victims of every herbivore, it has been discovered that they too have special defence systems. Among the most common are the calcification of the fronds or the production of toxic substances acting selectively on the various predators. The quantity of repellent compounds even increases within

C - Well known predators are the Serranidae, mainly represented by groupers (in the photo, the Epinephelus tauvina). Their hunting strategy, based on a quick spurt and rapid opening of the mouth to almost suck in the prey, is easily explained by the form of the mouths. This opens very wide and has a set of front teeth which, although small, are sharp and bent backwards to prevent the prey from escaping.

D - Boxfish are certainly among the most unusual fish. An example is this Acanthostracion polygonius of the Caribbean recognized by its rigid body, often with polygonal plates. The mouth is small with thick lips and conical or incisor-shaped teeth rounded at the point. They feed on benthic invertebrates such as ascidians, sponges, Alcyonarians and large quantities of algae.

E - Parrot fish are easily identified by their robust teeth, resembling a beak and fused in a sort of mosaic, forming four plates in all (two upper and two lower). At the back of the mouth behind the beak is a group of pharyngeal teeth similar to molars used to crumble the food, algae and fragments of corals broken off by the beak.

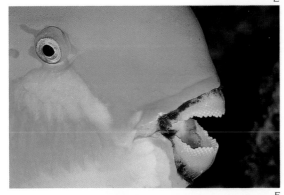

F - The large break in this brain coral, still white, reveals the recent passage of a group of parrot fish; close examination also shows the blows struck by single fish. Below water it is hard to mistake the sharp noises made by the beak of a parrot fish intent on feeding on the corals.

the same species according to the intensity of feeding on the part of herbivores. The most specialized carnivores on the reef must include the Chaetodontidae or butterflyfish and the Monacanthidae or file fish which devour the coral polyps seizing them in their fine teeth and mouths like tweezers. In fact the name "Chaetodontidae" means "teeth like bristles". Even the fire coral, one of the most untouchable organisms on the reef - at least for humans - has its admirers, namely the *Aluterus scriptus*, a Monacanthidae found near the tropics.

The drawing illustrates the characteristic behaviour of a pair of Pomacentrus (1) busy defending their garden of algae from other herbivorous fish. As has been clearly shown in research conducted on some coral reefs, the intensity of the aggressive reactions of damselfish towards other species is not triggered so much by the invasion of the territory but more by the feeding habits of the species concerned. Carangidae (2), parrotfish (3), butterfly (4), angelfish (7), surgeon (8), will even be attacked beyond the actual confines of the territory whereas carnivorous species such as blennies (5) and gobies (6), are allowed to penetrate undisturbed to the centre of the "cultivated" territory. Sometimes the aggressiveness of the damselfish is also directed at notoriously herbivorous invertebrates such as sea urchins.

A - Although butterflyfish tend usually to live alone or in pairs, they often group together mainly to better exploit the food resources and combat the aggressiveness of the larger or territorial fish. The species in the photo is the Chaetodon fasciatus, a butterflyfish typical of the Red Sea.

This diagram is based on the previous scene and serves to better illustrate the defensive behaviour of damselfish. The dotted and continuous lines refer respectively to the outermost and innermost boundaries of the territory. The crucial zone is, of course, the internal one and access is permitted only to carnivorous (in green) and therefore not rival species. Herbivorous fish (in red) are attacked as soon as they cross the safety boundary and blocked before they can penetrate further. The more similar the species' behaviour is to that of the damselfish, the more rapid and intense the aggressive reaction. To demonstrate how well developed the territorial instinct is, suffice to say that damselfish, less than 10 centimetres long, successfully manage to combat fish such as the much larger parrotfish.

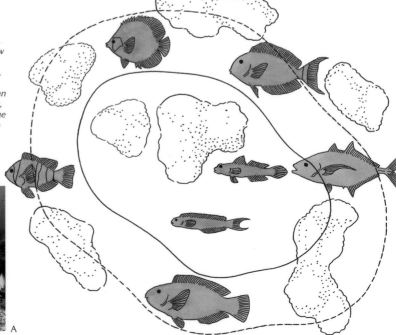

A

Another food reserve produced by coral in large quantities but scarcely heeded is the mucus that the Madrepore secretes as a reaction in unfavourable situations. Some Pomacentridae and Monacanthidae and even some Chaetodontidae have been seen removing the mucus concentrated between the walls of the corallites; many small fish also take advantage of the abundance of this food, rich in fats, found after the passage of a shoal of parrot fish. This mucus is a resource also for the so called planktivorous fish; constantly removed by the waves and currents, it mixes with the detritus and bacteria present in the water and is transformed into minute particles of a high nutritional value. On a reef even sponges become food for fish - surgeonfish, in particular, are very often principally responsible for the control of the local numbers of these invertebrates. In cases of specialized hunting such as that just described - but the example is applicable to many other types of resource - it has been observed that, as soon as the "energetic cost" of the search for nourishment becomes too high for the scarcity of the prey, the feeding conduct of the species changes, embracing a wider spectrum of prey until the sponges remaining regain a satisfactory density.
The countless species of invertebrates (in particular molluscs, crustaceans, worms and echinoderms) living in the crevices of the reef or buried in the sand are not merely an important food reserve for each other in various circumstances they are also a fundamental resource for numerous fish specifically adapted to a hunting of this type, calling for strong teeth and good swimming ability.

B

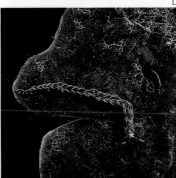

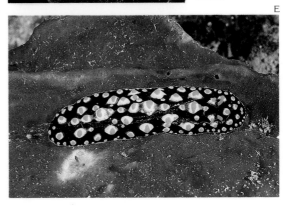

C

D

E

B - The coloured tufts indicating the presence of the sedentary polychaeta Spirobranchus giganteus or Christmas tree worm are none other than the branchia of these creatures, totally dependent on what the currents bring to them. The branchial tufts also serve to capture food and trap minute organisms and detritus with the plumed tentacles around the mouth.

C - The bright colouring of these Crinoids and blue starfish (Linckia laevigata) of the Pacific serve to warn possible predators of the poor taste of their flesh. Aposematic colouring (i.e. of warning) is found in numerous organisms on reefs and represents an effective system of defence.

D - The Eolids are nudibranch molluscs characterized by a thin and often elongated body, the back covered with rows of finger-shaped expansions. Their nourishment consists mostly in Hydrozoa, some colonies being visible in the lower half of the photo. Although their prey have stinging cells, these nudibranchs are capable of absorbing the defences of their victims and transfer them to the tip of their dorsal papillae.

E - The bright colours distinguishing nudibranchs (in the photo a Phyllidia) are a classic example of aposematic colouring, i.e. for warning purposes. Possible predators soon learn to avoid these small organisms as visible and easy to capture as they are impossible to eat. It is no coincidence that the main predators of these molluscs include nudibranchs themselves in whom the colouring instills no fear.

The Lethrinidae or emperors swim close to the bottom ready to avert the smallest indication of the presence of a hidden animal. Rays wave their wide pectoral fins raising great clouds of sand and uncovering molluscs and crabs; immediately seized upon, these are crushed by powerful teeth shaped like a grindstone; Lutjanidae and grouper, well aware of their strength, swim unhurriedly amid the intricate weave of reefs appearing and disappearing from the view of divers trying to follow them. Their swimming is in no way aggressive but their apparent laziness screens a thorough and constant inspection of the surrounding environment; any slip on the part of its inhabitants and these able predators will act like lightning. For this reason, their passage triggers the immediate disappearance of many small fish, always anxious to remain a safe distance from their potential enemies and never venturing too far from their refuges. Not always, however, does this reaction of flight occur and this would seem to indicate the existence of signals, imperceptible to man but well known in the fish world, by which the prey can tell whether a fish is hunting or simply passing by. Many pelagic fish (carangids, tuna, sharks) which habitually live along the walls of the reefs fronting the open sea are by nature carnivorous and often effect collective and coordinated hunting expeditions against shoals of the smallest fish. These tactics are used by carangids who surround shoals of fish, blocking their escape routes, and then attack systematically. Similar behaviour is certainly more profitable than solitary hunting as small fish in shoals may prove a less effective prey than would appear, the shoal constituting an excellent defence system. This is clearly demonstrated by the fact that more than 50% of fish live their youth in shoals and approximately 25% continue to do so as adults. Living in a shoal increases the probabilities of survival of the single fish and reduces those of success for a predator. The rapid

A - A Blue-spotted lagoon ray (Taeniura lymma) *raises the sediment on the sea bed in search of the invertebrates it feeds on.*

B - The Letrinidae (in the photo Monotaxis grandoculis) or Emperors usually swim close to the sea bed carefully scrutinizing the sandy areas in search of crustaceans, molluscs and other invertebrates.

C - Groupers are active predators though every species behaves differently: some prefer to wait in ambush in points of forced passage for fish, others swim around in the vicinity of their dens. Some hunt by day and others by night.

D - Lutjanidae, such as the Blue-striped snapper Lutjanus kasmira *common from the Red Sea to the Tuamotu islands, gather in shoals during the day. By night they scatter to hunt small fish and benthic invertebrates.*

E - Barracudas (Sphyraena sp.) are predators occupying the last rings of the reef food chain. They form dense shoals of sometimes hundreds of fish and swim compactly in the water in search of prey - shoals of smaller fish, such as sardines and anchovies.

dispersion of the members of a shoal which seems to open before the attack of a large carnivore and close immediately behind it may be an effective way to favour the survival of the single members as the predator does not know who to attack in the general but only apparently confused commotion. In these cases the main purpose of the hunting fish is apparently to identify the weakened fish, normally slower to recreate the shoal and,therefore, tending to remain isolated. On other occasions, the shoal forms on the approach of a predator. This is

E

F

F - Along the walls of a reef one often comes across groups of grey reef sharks (Carcharhinus amblyrhynchos), invariably shadowed by Lutjanidae, Letrinidae and large surgeon fish (Naso sp.) recognized by spines along the side of the caudal peduncle. In some areas where for some time the habit of feeding sharks has been introduced, these creatures rapidly approach divers, causing a fright that is not totally unjustified.

thought to be a deterrent determined by the mass of assembled fish which, it has been observed, in a situation of this kind swim very close together. The formation of shoals is not, however, a prerogative of planktivorous or carnivorous and predatory fish. On the contrary, in some species it represents an effective system aimed at better exploiting the resources and is also adopted by herbivorous fish with different techniques according to the environmental conditions. The *Acanthurus triostegus* surgeonfish for instance forms large columnar throngs to feed on the sea bottoms occupied by territorial rivals but, where the bottom is rougher and more varied and the interspecific competition reduced, the shoals take on a more extended form and have a purely defensive function.
One of the most characteristic methods of hunting, related to specific adaptations in form and colour (homomorphism and

G - The shoals of Carangids (Caranx sp.) swim in the waters around the outer fronts of the reefs, watching the movements of the shoals of smaller fish. During the hunting phase the fast Carangids behave like wolves; they surround the shoal of fish and push it towards the reef until all possibilities of escape vanish. Only at this point do the predators attack, moving to a coordinated plan.

homochromatism) is that of the fish who create ambushes. Examples are the crocodile and lizard fish or the Scorpaenidae and Antennaridae, the latter even having an artificial bait to attract the prey. Direct observation of the reef fish can also result in the discovery of temporary alliances between various species. Together they exploit the particular skills of one of the members of the temporary association. An emblematic example of this is the goat fish. During their wanderings these fish use their sensitive whiskers and snout to inspect sediments on the sea bed. They are often accompanied by opportunists such as Labridae, Lutjanidae and trumpet fish primed to seize upon the small fish and invertebrates set to flight but not directly threatened by the mullet.

To conclude, the method used by triggerfish to capture sea urchins is an example of how every attack strategy corresponds to one of defence and viceversa. To our eyes the long, poisonous spines of the diadema sea urchin certainly appear formidable but these arms are no obstacle to the cunning triggerfish. Particularly fond of echinoids, the Balistidae carefully grasps the spines of the sea urchin, drags it upwards away from the bottom and attacks it as it falls, from underneath where the unprotected mouth is located. If the resistance of the urchin cannot be won the triggerfish will resort to another more sophisticated technique which consists in blowing powerful jets of water at the base of the urchin until it is overturned and becomes harmless.

A

B

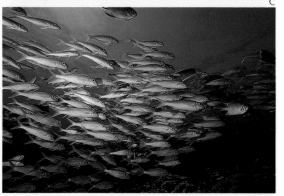

C

A - The shoals of fusilier fish (Caesio sp.) are sometimes so dense as to hide a diver from the sight of his companions. The compact nature of the shoal is one of the best forms of defence for otherwise helpless species.

B - A shoal of Pterocaesio tile, a species of fusilier fish (Caesionidae) common in the waters between the coasts of Eastern Africa and New Caledonia, swims in front of the photographer.

C - During the day the Yellowfin goatfish (Mulloidichthys vanicolensis) unite in large groups which swim lazily along the reef, often remaining in the column of water. By night this gregarious behaviour is abandoned and the single fish scatter to inspect the sandy sea bottom and detritus in search of the invertebrates they feed on and find thanks to sensitive barbels, organs of both touch and taste.

D - Lizardfish (Synodontidae) are tendentially sedentary and hunt by sight relying on the camouflaged colouring of their body - often buried in the sediment with just the eyes and part of the mouth emerging. As seen in the photo and from the Labridae protruding from its mouth this is a successful hunting strategy.

E - Crocodile fish (Platycephalidae family) owe their name to the long flattened snout and well-developed jaws. These fish also lie in ambush on the bottom, sometimes half buried. Their prey are mainly crustaceans supplemented by imprudent fish swimming past the mouth of the Platycephalidae and captured with a rapid snap.

D

E

H

H - A far from conspicuous colour and a body shaped to blend in with the uneven sea bed are essential features of sedentary creatures such as the Antennariidae. Their skill as predators is increased by a long filament above the mouth terminating in a growth. This is proof that nature invented the fishing line before man and serves as a bait to attract prey.

F
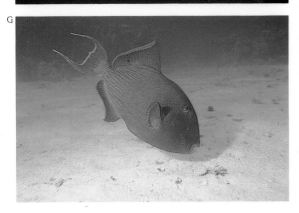

G

F - The elongated and comical contours of these cornetfish (Fistularia commersonii) hardly seem those of a dangerous predator. In actual fact, this long fish is a threat to the smallest fish; it drifts close to them with the current or hides behind larger but harmless fish. Once close to its prey the cornet fish opens its mouth wide and rapidly sucks in the fish or crustacean.

G - The strange behaviour of this triggerfish (Pseudobalistes fuscus) is reminiscent of the tale of the bad wolf and the three little pigs. Just as the wolf tried to blow down the house of the little pigs and eat them, so too the triggerfish can blow powerful jets of water onto the sea bottom to uncover prey or overturn and render harmless the sea urchins they love to eat.

REPRODUCTION

Although nutrition strategies are important for survival of the individual fish, those of reproduction are vital. Highly variable as can easily be imagined, they are so complex as to make all attempts at generalization or synthesis difficult. Although there are species which lay eggs on the sea bottom and later take care of the young, or species which disperse their eggs among the sediments or fix them wrapped in protective casing to a substratum, almost all fish reproduce by tiny pelagic eggs (1-2 mm) which usually open after a week. The size of the larvae depends on that of the eggs and they are very different from the parents, immediately becoming plankton. Mingling among the millions of other smaller organisms, the fish larvae grow to maturity and acquire the characteristics of the adults, this often only at sexual maturity. Sexual reproduction is the rule for fish, but matters are complicated in their world by the existence of hermaphroditism. Even though most species have different sexes, at least a hundred or so are hermaphroditic. As they grow they undergo a sex change for a phenomenon known as sequential hermaphroditism. This change may be from male to female (protandrous) or from female to male (protogynous). Labridae, Serranidae, Pomacentridae and Scaridae are typical cases of sex change, a phenomenon involving not only modifications in the physiology and internal anatomy but also in the external appearance with transformations of colour which, in the past, led experts to believe that the male and female of the same species belonged to different species.
This sex change is particularly complicated in parrotfish as some species begin as females and then become males and in others a subject may remain male for its entire life span. This means that in a family there are four different increasingly conspicuous colour phases: female, primary male, intersexual and secondary male.

A

D

A - The delicate mucous ribbon contains hundreds of tiny balls - the eggs of the red Spanish dancer (Hexabranchus sanguineus). Frequently nudibranch eggs adopt the characteristic colouring of their species.

B - The reproduction of holothurians is always an extraordinary spectacle for those lucky enough to witness it. Under the influence of invisible but powerful chemical messengers dispersed in the water over large areas, all the holothurians of a certain zone, seemingly drawn by invisible threads, will with perfect synchronization straighten up in the water to expel eggs and spermatozoa.

C - The cloud enveloping this large Demospongiae is made up of male gametes which, when scattered in the water, can ride with the currents to the eggs contained in other sponges and fertilize them.

D - The large ramifications of the Pterogorgia ancieps serve as a substratum to which large ovigerous capsules adhere; this curious "object", more similar to a product manufactured by man than a natural one, probably belongs to this category.

Although this has created some systematical problems there is no doubt that colour and dimensions have made it possible to distinguish, albeit with some approximation, the sexes of the various species, as the larger, coloured specimens invariably being male. The form of reproduction in Scaridae again varies greatly. Sometimes a pair form, almost exclusively the prerogative of the largest males, in others reproductive groups of not yet fully developed males and females come together.

Reproduction in these circumstances is quite simple and involves 3-15 fish at a time; in turn these abandon their shoal and rise close to the surface where the gametes are expelled. Reproduction in couples is preceded by elaborate courting on the part of a male who has first marked off his territory. As soon as a group of conspecific fish passes in the vicinity the male shows off by swimming with all its fins outstretched, pointing first upwards and then downwards performing zig zags. Should its movements attract the attention of a female and this approaches, the movements of the male become

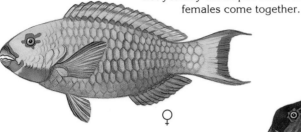

♀

Steephead parrotfish
Scarus gibbus

♂

♀

Rusty parrotfish
Scarus ferrugineus

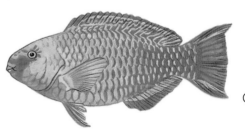

♂

♀

Bullethead parrotfish
Scarus sordidus

♂

swifter until the female also joins in. The couple swims slantingly towards the surface, separates on descent to reunite at the centre of the territory. The repetition of these rhythmic movements plays a vital role in the synchronization of the expulsion of the gametes; as in the previous case, this occurs close to the surface. Despite the variation in the behaviour leading up to reproduction, it has been seen that among the various species of Scaridae there is a considerable analogy in the choice of period and place elected for reproduction. These fish seem to prefer the outer faces of reefs and the period of high tides when currents capable of carrying away the fertilized eggs mingled with plankton are more likely to form. Similar conduct is also found in many surgeonfish of the Pacific which reproduce in areas characterized by constant currents directed towards the open sea. The sexually mature fish come together close to the surface and along the external slope of the reef to swim close-packed performing large loops. At regular intervals 3-5 subjects rise rapidly to the surface and, after having expelled the gametes, return to the shoal. Groupers, protogynous hermaphroditic fish, forego their solitary habits to form shoals at the time of reproduction. Among the most interesting and best known cases is that of the Nassau grouper (*Epinephelus striatus*): towards the end of January these gather off the Bahamas in preordained places to form shoals of up to 30,000 fish, some having covered more than 25 kilometres to meet and celebrate their fertility rites. The members of the Serranidae, related to groupers (subfamily Epinephelinae), are members of the subfamily Serraninae, according to the most recent classifications, and synchronous hermaphrodites. This means that every fish behaves simultaneously as a male and a female and its sexual glands, a mixture of ovaries and testicles are called "ovotestis". A classical example of synchronous hermaphroditism is the *Hypoplectrus unicolor* of the Caribbean. This fish lives solitary

A

B

C

A - Despite having adapted perfectly to many aspects of marine life, turtles (the photograph shows a couple busy in amorous rituals) must necessarily leave the water to lay their eggs.

B - A pair of Plectorhinchus orientalis *swims close to a coral formation, showing the distinctive striped colouring and the black spots on the yellow fins.*

C - Groupers are protogynous fish, that is to say that these creatures change from females to males during their growth. Large groupers are therefore always males.

during the day and forms pairs at sunset to reproduce, the male rising towards the surface wrapped around the "female". This species is also of interest for another reason. Although its specific name is "unicolor" there are at least ten varieties clearly recognizable by their colours. Once believed to be different species, they were then thought to be varieties of the same species. An indication of the progress yet to be made in the definition of the inhabitants of the

sea comes from the fact that some experts have now returned to the conviction that these are different species, bioacoustic research having revealed that each variety uses a different language to communicate with its equals. That fish are not mute has been known for some time and the fact that intraspecific communication can prove useful when the pair forms is also shown by some Caribbean ray's beam of the *Stegastes* genus; although they become almost identical in the reproduction period, they can be distinguished quite easily from the sounds emitted during courtship. The formation of the couples is a fairly common phenomenon in butterflyfish and in at least a dozen species this union seems to be lasting. Fixed pairs have been studied for periods of up to three years and the members, according to observations, seemed capable of recognizing each other. After a period of separation, usually

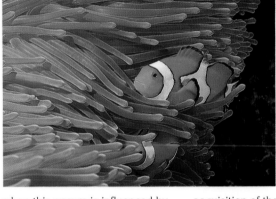

D - A large number of butterflyfish (in the photo two Chaetodon semilarvatus) *may live together in stable couples for several years.*

E - When two butterflyfish are observed together it is very often not merely a momentary association for reproduction purposes or defence of the territory. In the picture it is possible to see two Chaetodon fasciatus *swimming close to the reef.*

F - A pair of Amphiprion percula *is hidden in the long tentacles of their host.*

G - Clownfish live in pairs closely associated with sea anemones. The female is the largest of the two members of the pair. Curiously, if the female is lost the surviving male changes sex and becomes female.

caused by the search for food in different areas, the two members of the couple performed a particular type of dance which, described in human terms, seemed the equivalent of a display of joy for the reunion. Some angelfish of the Atlantic, the *Pomacanthus arcuatus* and the *Pomacanthus paru* also live in stable couples, at least until outside factors intervene to separate them. Couples stable for up to three years have been observed in clown fish (*Amphiprion* genus). They can recognize their partner so well that they will chase it violently if it is in some way transformed experimentally, e.g. altering its markings. Even more interesting is the fact that the formation of the pair in these fish depends on hormonal factors but its preservation is bound to a cascade reaction of social inhibition. Clown fish undergo a sex change but

when this occurs is influenced by the presence or absence of a female, the dominating subject. Normally every clown fish pair lives in an anemone, accompanied by a variable number of subadults, depending on the dimensions of the anemone. Although the male is smaller than the female, it is always larger than all the subadults which it drives away as soon as they come near, thus keeping them in a subordinate position. When, for some reason, the female disappears, the male of the couple undergoes a rapid sex change and in satellite subadults battle for the

acquisition of the role of dominating male. The Pomacentridae family, that of clownfish, also presents different reproduction conduct. Some solitary species accept the presence of subjects of the opposite sex only at the moment of reproduction and in some gregarious species a considerable number of subjects unite to defend a common territory, usually a ramified coral colony, against all the other fish.
The social control of the sex change is even more obvious in other species. The most famous of

A

differs greatly. Some species reproduce all year and some only in limited periods. For the majority reproduction seems to take place during the night, preferably at those times of the year when the waters are calmer. This choice seems determined by the reduced presence of possible predators and the need to favour fertilization of the eggs. As this occurs in open water excessive turbulence can negatively affect it. The phases of the moon also seem to have

A - The dense clusters of Pseudanthias invariably populating the slopes of coral reefs from the surface down to thirty metres or so are only apparently chaotic. If carefully observed they are seen to be composed of immature fish, non territorial females and males having their own territory and a harem of females.

B - The male anthias are easily identified by the long ray situated on the front part of the dorsal fin.

the cleaner fish of the Indo-Pacific, the *Labroides dimidiatus*, forms groups consisting in one male and six or more females. The females make up a harem and the male may mate daily with each of them. If the male is eliminated the largest female changes sex and takes on the male role. The change is very fast. Male behaviour appears after just a few hours although the reproductive organs (testicles instead of ovaries) start to function after 10 days. Harems are present also in the Anthias (e.g. *Pseudanthias squamipinnis*), the smaller and less coloured subjects being female and the larger ones, distinguished by their brighter colours and very long first rays of the dorsal fin, are all males. Among these, however, some dominant ones live close to strategical points of the reef while the others remain farther away. The angelfish *Centropyge bicolor* also have harems and a socially determined sexual change; a single male controls a territory accompanied by about ten females, reproducing with them practically every day, at dusk. It is sometimes aided in this by a subordinate male who may take its place should the dominant male disappear. In other cases if the number of females present becomes too high, the dominant male may divide its territory, occupying only a part with a group of females and leaving the new male to take over the remaining space with its own harem. The period in which reproduction takes place also

B

an important influence as reproduction has been seen to coincide with the full moon in numerous species. Lutjanidae, many groupers, surgeonfish, Apogonidae, Pomacentridae and triggerfish all have lunar cycles. Not always are the eggs abandoned and left to the currents and the resources offered by plankton. Some species lay their eggs on the sea bottom as is typical of the Pomacentridae (*Chromis, Abdudefduf, Dascyllus, Amphiprion* genera); these territorial fish clean the area chosen for the eggs and care for them oxygenating them with their fins, removing any detritus covering them and keeping away possible predators, even if larger, by attacking them violently. Generally speaking, in fish characterized by this type of reproduction, the initiative is taken by the males which, within their territory, mark off a particular area for the eggs. On its own territory the male parades itself in courting activities aimed at attracting any

females passing in groups.
The courting rite may be repeated
several times so a male may
find himself guarding eggs laid
by various females. Blennies
and gobies behave in a similar
manner whereas the Apogonidae
display even more obvious
parental care as the males carry
the eggs in their mouths until
they open, and needlefish and
sea horse (Syngnathiform) males
protect the fertilized eggs in
a capacious incubating pouch
until they open.

E

C

D

*C - Colonies of
ramified Madrepores
represent the ideal
habitat for green
damselfish
(Chromis viridis).
The fish unite to
form dense
conglomerations,
each electing a
Madrepore as its
territory and driving
all other species or
groups away.*

*D - Crinoids have
separate sexes
although these are
not easy to identify.
At the moment of
reproduction
spermatozoa and
tiny eggs are
released in mass
into the water
where fertilization
takes place.
The fertilized eggs
adhere to the arms
of the female until a
larva forms.
This initially leads
a planktonic life,
then metamorphosis
takes place and it
moves to the sea
bottom where, at
first, it remains fixed
by a small peduncle
which will later
break. This
anatomical structure
brings to mind the
erect stem by which
sea lilies, distant
sessile and not
vagile ancestors of
Crinoids, remained
fixed to the sea bed.*

*E - Parrotfish (in the
photograph a group
of* Bolbometopon
muricatum) *change
sex during their
growth. Initially
female, the
parrotfish become
male when they
grow. This sex
change is also
accompanied in
most cases by a
change in colour.*

SYMBIOSIS AND OTHER RELATIONSHIPS

The high density of species living on reefs has gradually led to the appearance of interaction between the different species which have established almost obligatory symbiotic relationships although the term symbiosis is now considered to broad to be a precise classification of behaviour.

The term symbiosis is increasingly being replaced by the more exact one of mutualism, emphasizing a relationship in which both the host and the symbiont draw mutual benefit. A particularly successful example of mutualistic symbiosis is that of clownfish *(Amphiprion* genus*)* and their anemones.

As the symbiont of such a well equipped host in defensive terms, there is no doubt that the clownfish enjoys obvious advantages.

The most important is that of being totally protected from possible predators as shown by the fact that clown fish deprived of their anemone are soon devoured. Another advantage is that of enjoying the leftovers from the anemone's meals as despite it being almost impossible for it to move, the anemone is a voracious predator. This combined with the apparent inertia of the anemone led in the past to the conjecture that the association were not mutualistic, but merely commensalistic.

In actual fact, prolonged observation has shown that clownfish are capable of keeping the anemone's most common predators, butterflyfish such as *Chaetodon fasciatus*, away. In some cases the mutualistic association is very close: the *Amphiprion nigripes* species lives exclusively with *Hecteractis magnifica* whereas *Amphiprion frenatus* and *Premnas biaculeatus* are always associated with *Entacmea quadricolor*.

Far less specific are the habits of *Amphiprion clarkii* which can be found amid the tentacles of ten species of anemones; the most hospitable anemone is certainly *Heteractis crispa*, associated with 14 species of *Amphiprion*.

B

C

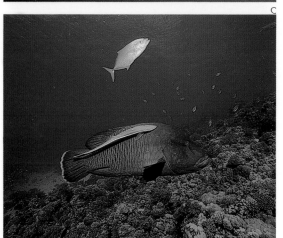

A - The need to adhere to a larger organism sometimes entails sacrifices, as in the case of this overturned remora (Echeneis naucrates) that is upside down, lying on a nurse shark (Nebrius Ferrugineus) head. In fact, remoras usually cling to the belly of larger fish by means of their sucker.

B - A formation of remoras adheres to the belly of a large manta (Manta birostris). Remoras, once considered parasites of other fish, are actually commensal symbionts feeding both on the leftovers of the associate species and on what they find as they are carried through the water. Remoras are indeed useful as they can also feed on the external parasites of their hosts.

C - The remora adheres to its host by means of the dorsal fin transformed into a sucker; an oval organ with two rows of parallel lamellae *between which a vacuum can be formed. In this picture it is possible to observe a remora swimming close to a Napoleon wrasse (Cheilinus undulatus).*

D

organisms such as the large nudibranchs of the *Hexabranchus sanguineus* species better known as the Spanish dancer and generally associated with the *Periclimenes imperator*.

In these cases of commensalism only one of the two species involved benefits directly, the other not drawing particular gain. Once considered a form of forced commensalism and today described as a mutualistic symbiosis true and proper is the association of crustaceans and fish. Swimming close to the coral sand bed it is not rare, in the crevices at the base of the corals

E

One aspect has always aroused great curiosity, namely how clownfish manage to survive the stinging tentacles of the anemone as their protection is neither total nor permanent. If a clownfish moves away for some time it loses its immunity and may be killed by contact with the stinging tentacles of the anemone.

The symbiosis is possible only because every clownfish can gradually accustom itself to its own anemone - and apparently that one alone - by increasing the thickness of its mucus covering by as much as fourfold. This prevents the anemone from perceiving the clown fish as extraneous and it can thus penetrate without risk between the tentacles of its host. Clownfish are not, however, alone in exploiting the defence offered by the anemones. Some Labridae (e.g. *Halichoeres garnoti* and *Thalassoma bifasciatum*), Pomacentridae *(Dascyllus aruanus)* and even parrotfish form mutualistic associations with anemones, though only at the young stage.

Also guests of anemones are some invertebrates such as the prawns of the *Periclimenes* genus, as common in the Indo-Pacific as in the Caribbean, and found, depending on species, also on holothurians, starfish (e.g. *Periclimenes soror* and *Linckia laevigata*), between the tentacles of corals (e.g. *Periclimenes longicarpus* and *Plerogyra sinuosa*) and even on quite mobile

F

D - The association between clownfish (in the photograph Amphiprion perideraion) *and sea anemones is a classic example of mutualistic symbiosis. In some cases other Pomacentridae, such as the young of the domino damselfish* (Dascyllus trimaculatus), *associate temporarily with a sea anemone for defence purposes.*

E - Two clownfish (Amphiprion perideraion) *shelter in their sea anemone host.*

F - This clownfish (Amphiprion nigripes) *peeps out from the tentacles of a sea anemone; the fish rarely strays from this safe refuge.*

A - The clownfish (Amphiprion sp.) are rather small, in adults their dimensions vary from 9 to 16 centimetres.

B - Even this clownfish (Amphipron ocellaris) is sheltering in the anemone chosen as its residence.

C - A pair of spiny clownfish (Premnas biaculeatus) is observing the photographer. This species has two sturdy conspicuous spines below its eyes; it lives in association with the sea anemones of the (Entacmaea quadricolor) species whose tentacles are swollen at the tips.

D - Clownfish manage to live amidst the stinging tentacles of anemones thanks to specific adaptations. Every clownfish must accustom itself gradually to contact with the tentacles of the anemone, slowly increasing the thickness of its covering mucous. This thick layer prevents the anemone from recognizing the clownfish as extraneous and striking it with its stinging cells. In the image you can see an Amphiprion clarkii among the tentacles of "its" sea anemone.

or in dens dug in the sediments, to observe the simultaneous presence of fish, usually gobies, and crustaceans, mostly prawns of the Alfeidae family characterized by having one chela better developed than the other. In these cases, and always for defence purposes, the two members of the association share some of their special qualities. The nearly blind prawns are able diggers and quickly prepare a deep den, then offered to their host; above all they keep it clean, like small, untiring bulldozers turning out the sediments constantly caving in. The fish act as guards posted on the bottom close to the entrance to the den and keep an eye on what is happening. In the event of danger, the goby quickly seeks refuge in the hole to re-emerge with the prawn when the alarm has ceased. The members of the pair are always in contact and use specific warning signals - the goby waves its tail and the prawn moves its antennae.

A different type of association is established between crabs and gobies living together between the branches of corals. Their cohabitation is not clearly definable as it appears that the fish uses the crab as an armoured barrier between the outside world and its refuge. The association is not, however, easy and requires a certain period of adjustment as frequently the crabs chosen as "guardians" eat the fish if these are very small. Of a different nature are the associations in which the fish act as tenants in various invertebrates. In this field sponges, especially in the Caribbean where Poriferae are extremely abundant, have a prominent role as at least 14 species of sponges are known to offer refuge to more than 30 different species of fish in all, gobiidae being in the clear majority. Other gobies, as mentioned on the subject of camouflage, usually live on the branches of Gorgonians or associated with crinoids.

Much more fascinating is the association between Carapidae and holothurians. The Indo-Pacific species *Encheliophis homei* lives in both bivalves and echinoderms including starfish of the *Culcita* genus into which they can penetrate.

The *Carapus bermudensis* has the same habits living in the shells of molluscs or in the bodies of holothurians, emerging at night to feed. The practices of cleaning exercised both by fish and crustaceans is one of the best studied social relationships and practically essential. This is a mutualistic symbiosis in which the cleaner draws sustenance from the parasites and pieces of skin eliminated from the host fish and these greatly benefit from this liberation.

Cleaning fish belong basically to the family of Labridae (*Labroides*, the best known, and *Thalassoma*

E

F

genera and species such as *Bodianus rufus*, *Halichoeres bivattatus*). Occasionally some Chaetodontidi and Pomacentridae act as cleaners, but only when young and recognizable as such by other fish for their markings, totally different, of course, from those of the adults.

The cleaning procedure always takes place in the same place or station, although the cleaner may change, and is preceded by a complex rite and the exchange of recognition signals. The fish wishing to be cleaned approaches the "cleaning station" adopting a series of poses which unmistakably demonstrate its intentions. Sometimes it takes on a vertical position with the head upwards or downwards or it remains immobile with its gill covers and mouth wide open. Often this behaviour is accompanied by changes in colouring. In response to these signals, the cleaning fish *Labroides dimidiatus* approaches swimming to and fro to show its light blue and black colouring which allows

G

H

E - The crustaceans of the Periclimenes genus are in many cases commensal parasites of sea anemones or corals. Between the tentacles or in the cavities of these stinging organisms or hard invertebrates the prawns find a protection similar to that offered to clownfish.

F - The transparency of the shell of prawns associated with anemones and corals (in the photograph a detail of the coral of the Plerogyra genus) makes it extemely difficult to see them because of the different illumination below the surface of the sea. As well as a place of refuge, anemones and corals can also become a resource for crustaceans which feed on their mucous.

G - Gobies and prawns are one of the best known mutualistic associations on coral reefs. The photograph shows a goby of the Amblyeleotris genus and a prawn of the Alpheus genus - having one of their two chelae better developed - peeping out of the same den. Of the two halves of the symbiosis, the fish gives the alarm in the event of danger and the prawn, having very poor eyesight, digs and keeps the den clear for both.

H - Blennies are typically associated with holes, either cavities in rocks or corals, the dens of other creatures or their empty shells.

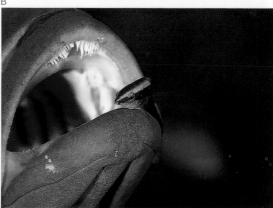

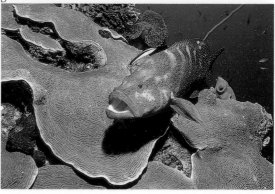

A - In certain parts of a reef divers soon notice the presence of small black and blue fish swimming busily around larger fish. These are cleaning stations where cleaner fish (in the photograph the most typical of these, a Labroides dimidiatus *is busy cleaning a redmouth grouper* Aethaloperca rogaa) *eliminate the parasites infesting other fish.*

B, C - The relationship between fish and cleaner fish is so close and the latters' work so greatly appreciated that the Labroides dimidiatus *can penetrate without fear into the mouth of a fish that could easily eat them in one bite. The faith in the ability of the cleaner is such that the grouper even accepts the cleaning process impassively in a delicate area such as the gills.*

D - Fish approaching cleaning stations show their good will to the cleaner fish by remaining immobile with mouth, gills and fins open. Often the position of the body is accompanied by variations in colour and these are another sign of invitation to the cleaners.
The importance of these small fish is such that the number of fish species on a stretch of reef will decrease rapidly and the number of sick fish rise sharply if they are eliminated.

other fish to recognize it. Subsequently the cleaner proceeds to inspect the host close up and eliminates parasites, food residue and pieces of rotting skin. It obtains much of its food in this way. The importance of these cleaning stations along the reef is such that if the cleaner fish are experimentally eliminated, the whole fish population of the area suffers a drastic reduction.
The function of *Labroides dimidiatus* and the other congenerics (*Labroides bicolor, Labroides pectoralis, Labroides phthirophagus*) is undertaken in the Caribbean where this species is absent, by gobies, in particular *Gobiosoma oceanops* and *Gobiosoma evelynae* which have very similar colouring. Indeed the resemblance between Labridae and gobies is so marked that in the aquarium the fish of the Pacific recognize gobies immediately as cleaners and fish of the Caribbean allow *Labroides* to approach them without hesitation. For this reason some experts have suggested that Labridae of the *Labroides* genus were present in the Caribbean region until the waters cooled during the Ice Age and they became extinct.
The knowledge, or rather the memory, of the specific colouring seems to have remained in the fish cleaned thus offering a selective advantage to subjects with the same or similar colouring.
This convergence is an excellent example of the possible effects of biological factors on evolution or the conservation of forms and behaviour in a species.
The cleaning activity is not, however, exclusive to fish. Brightly coloured crustaceans, mainly red and white, also clean fish e.g. *Stenopus hispidus, Lysmata amboinensis* or *Hippolysmata grabhami*. These small prawns also have cleaning stations, often placed near corals or anemones where they usually live; to attract fish they move their long antennae and swim to and fro.
The fish recognize these signals and trustingly approach remaining immobile with their mouths and gill covers wide open while the

E - Cleaning organisms are also found among crustaceans. Many prawns associate with cleaner fish or replace them in cleaning operations as seen in photographs showing prawns associated with a large moray (Gymnothorax javanicus). The prawns are operating on the head, close to the gills and the mouth that the big fish keeps in opened in order to have a "good job" done.

F - A Sabre squirrelfish (Sargocentron spiniferum) stays motionless in order to let a prawn complete its job. Even if this fish feeds on this kind of small crustaceans, it would never damage the prawn that is eliminating the parasites infesting its skin.

crustaceans seek out and devour the parasites on their skin, in their mouth and in the branchial chambers. These prawns are so taken up by the cleaning activity that it is sometimes extended to divers who, unknowingly halting near a cleaning station, see small prawns approaching to commence immediately their cleaning operations on the fingers of the astounded divers.

E

F

G - Cleaner fish and prawns have different and specialized mansions to absolve. The first ones take care of the cleaning of teeth and skin; the others have more delicate mansions, like cleaning eyes and gills. In the picture a prawn is "operating" around the eyes of a red mouth grouper (Aethaloperca rogaa).

H, I - Even the coral grouper (Cephalopholis miniata) often stops in the "cleaning areas" in order to be cleaned from the fastidious parasites.

G

I

H

CAMOUFLAGE

Animal marking is a most fascinating topic and coral reef inhabitants are no exception, colour and form - visual impact - being of vital importance. It must, nonetheless, be stressed that colour, as for the other aspects dealt with thus far, cannot be considered separately from the other elements in fish biology. Certainly, no one can fail to see that colour plays an important role in both defence and attack mechanisms, as too in reproduction and social relationships, or in territorial disputes and that the variety and complexity of facts can often only be clearly deciphered with the aid of multiple interpretation. In a marine world primarily dominated by light, it is easy to understand the specific meaning acquired by colours, even the most obvious, especially when used as camouflage. Whether serving for hunting or for defence, camouflage is one of the most effective forms

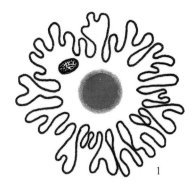

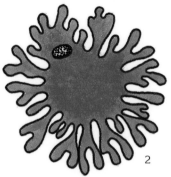

of adaptation connected with the survival of a species and all types satisfy the same requirement: invisibility. One of the classical examples of camouflage is that of the stone fish (Synanceia verrucosa) considered an absolute maestro in this art for the total fusion of form and conduct. Stocky and compact, with an uneven body studded with algae and other epibiont organisms, the stone fish, if one actually manages to see it, resembles a piece of coral rock covered with encrustations. Its camouflage is favoured by total immobility, as important a factor as appearance. One has to go very close and clearly show that it has been seen before a stone fish will move away with an angry start. The same technique is used by scorpion fish (Scorpaenopsis sp.), the Antenariidae, crocodilefish and sole; the successful camouflage of the latter depends not only on its ability to bury itself beneath the sand but also on certain specialized cells, chromotophores, used by this fish to change colour,

Chromatophore cross section.
The colours and variations in colouring in fish depend on special optic phenomena such as reflection, refraction and irridescence or specialized cells called chromatophores. The granules of pigment contained by these selectively absorb and reflect light.
The chromatophores have various names according to the colour of the pigments contained: erythrophores (red), xanthophores (yellow), melanophores (black).
The concentration of pigments at the centre of the chromatophore (1) gives the fish a paler colouring than when the pigments are scattered (2) all over the cell.

A - Stonefish (Synanceia sp.) are one of the greatest dangers of the coral reef. Their perfect camouflage and the large, sturdy dorsal fins connected to glands containing a poison more toxic than that of a cobra make them a more insidious menace than sharks. Only with long experience or special attention can one see a stonefish on the sea bed, its most striking features being the eyes and the shape of the mouth.

B - The Scorpaenidae of the Scorpaenopsis genus trust in their camouflage and are easily approached on the condition that the diver see them before making any sudden movements such to put them to flight.

A

B

adapting it to that of the surrounding sea bed.

Equally skilled sea chameleons are the octopus; they make themselves invisible by rapidly changing the colour and appearance of their body which may become sand, rock, algae - not only in colour but also in texture, with the manifestation of fine granulation, or other growths. Even apparently uncoloured fish such as the large pelagic predators (carangids, tuna, sharks) actually have colours perfectly matching their living requirements.

Thanks to a phenomenon called counter-shading, bluish-black backs and white or silvery bellies make these fish almost invisible when observed in the column of water from above or below, blending either with the darkness of the depths or with the light coming from the surface.

Camouflage does not, however, consist in resembling the surrounding environment alone. It is also trying to make the body disappear with "somatolytic"

C - *Leaf scorpionfish* (Taenionotus triacanthus) *are among the strangest of the Scorpaenidae. Not only do they resemble an admiral's cocked hat but at regular intervals they can change their epidermis, making it swell up until it breaks. The compressed, high form of their body allows them to sway like an algae drifting with the current. In this way they can approach their prey without arousing suspicion and swallow it with a rapid snap.*

D - *The blue spotted lagoon ray* (Taeniura lymma) *sometimes loves to bury itself in the sediment leaving the eyes and slits of the spiracles behind them jutting out to allow the water to reach the gills.*

E- *The Platycephalidae or crocodilefish are typical inhabitants of sandy seabeds and detritus where they bury themselves ready to surprise their prey.*

F- *The Pleuronectidae, comprising soles, flounders and turbot, are true flat fish, so well adapted to life on the seafloor that both their eyes have moved to just one side of the body. These fish are renowned for their camouflage ability. Their chromatophores are capable of perfectly imitating all types of sea bed and when this does not suffice they bury themselves.*

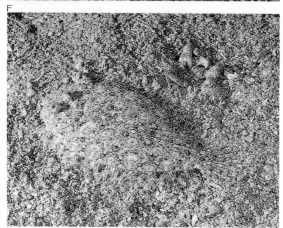

markings, i.e. those capable of breaking up the whole of the animal changing the apparent contours with patches, waves and streaking. In this way the eye of the potential enemy or possible prey, and even more so that of the scuba diver, fails to reconstruct the overall image of the animal, distracted by conspicuous marks, seemingly isolated and part of a far broader context than the body of a fish. Thus, the bright colours which have the effect of an advertising placard on humans and the contrasting patterns of their arrangement serve, in actual fact, to make the animal illegible. A striking case is that of the long nosed hawkfish *(Oxycirrhites typus)*; its red and white chequerboard markings, clearly visible in an underwater photo, prove ideal to conceal the fish when, as is its custom, it rests on a Gorgonian. The intersecting branches of the Gorgonians and the gaps created between them perfectly match the colours of the hawkfish making immediate identification difficult. Very similar

A

B

A - The bronze bluey body of the grey reef shark (Carcharhinus amblyrhynchos) allows it to disappear in the blue and reappear suddenly close to its prey.

B - The stripes running across the sides of these barracuda (Sphiraena qenie) may serve to favour the union of the shoal during transfers.

C

D

E

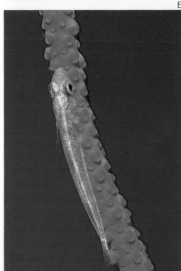

C - A tiny pixy hawkfish (Cirrhitichthys oxycephalus) hidden in a tangle of gorgonian branches.

D - The best known member of the Cirrhitidae family is the longnose hawkfish (Oxycirrhites typus). Its red and white chequerboard colouring hides the fish totally when resting, as is its custom, on gorgonian branches. It is not easy to see this species as it will swim quickly away from a diver, mockingly resting on the other side of the gorgonian.

is the case of the small Pterois; its dark and light patches and bands together with the distinct long rays of the pectoral and dorsal fins seem expressly designed to camouflage the fish among Gorgonians.
Form, colour and conduct combine to favour survival.
A shining example is that of trumpetfish *(Aulostomus sp.)*; although they can grow to up to a metre in size, they are able to make themselves almost invisible by remaining immobile with their head pointing downwards beside clusters of Gorgonians, waving in synchronization in the currents waiting for some other fish to seek momentary shelter in the vicinity. With just a few imperceptible flicks of the fin the fish moves in, opening its mouth, and in a flash sucks in the prey.
This strange fish, elongated and apparently harmless, is a skilled predator applying the "Trojan horse" technique underwater. It is often to be seen swimming concealed by the body of larger

E - On first sight, sea whip gorgonians do not seem a suitable refuge for fish. Nonetheless some small gobies (Bryaninops sp.) have turned this unusual habitat into their ideal ecological niche.

notoriously inoffensive species such as parrotfish, thus able to approach its prey without creating alarm.

Other species with thin, elongated bodies such as needle fish, remain hidden, weaving between the corals or swaying with the algae and filiform Gorgonians; razor fish *(Aeoliscus strigatus)* are even more specialized as they remain immobile and vertical between the prickles of sea urchins becoming almost invisible thanks to their longitudinal streaking, parallel to the spines. Camouflage marking is not always so evident and unmistakable to the eye of man. Round patches, known as ocellis for their shape, are, for instance, one of the most obvious characteristics of many tropical species which develop them for defence purposes together with dark bands hiding the eyes.

The presence of these two manifest markings springs from the need to protect delicate organs such as the eyes from attacks by small but specialized predators by distracting their attention.

A singular case of ocellar markings is that of the comet fish *Calloplesiops altivelis.*

When threatened this fish takes refuge in the closest crevice, protecting its head but leaving its tail and the end of its back with the ocellar patch sticking out.

There is such an incredible resemblance with the head of a large moray *(Gymnothorax meleagris)* as to discourage other fish from proceeding with their attack. A highly unusual type of camouflage, known as Batesian mimicry, makes two systematically totally different species so alike as to be indistinguishable in their environment.

Among the best known examples is the cleaner fish *Labroides dimidiatus* and its mimic represented by the blenny *Aspidontus taeniatus*, a voracious predator The latter imitates the cleaner fish perfectly both in colouring, identical to that of the most common local cleaner, and in its movements. Because of this unbelievable resemblance the prey

F

G

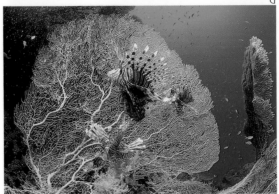

H

I

F - The branches of gorgonians observed through the macro lens of an underwater camera reveal countless tiny inhabitants which pass their entire existence in this microcosm. These two gobies of the Bryaninops *genus (the female, larger, is at the bottom) are inspecting a gorgonian branch in search of the ideal place to lay eggs. When the site has been chosen some species then systematically eliminate the gorgonian polyps.*

G - The large fans of gorgonians form a natural barrier against the currents; behind this any fish which are not great lovers of rough waters such as cobrafish (Pterois miles) can hide or take shelter.

H - The resemblance between fish and the predominant type of sea bed is manifested clearly by this needlefish (fam. Singnatidae), its form and colour almost perfectly reflecting that of the blade of eel-grass above it.

I - It is sometimes difficult to identify fish by their colour when different geographical breeds exist. This photograph shows fish of the Chaetodon unimaculatus *species typical of the Indian Ocean and the western Indo-Malay archipelago. They are all yellow, those of the Pacific yellow and white.*

A, D - The small size of gobies (Bryaninops sp.) and their almost total lack of defences would make them the ideal prey for many organisms. Gobies successfully overcome this inferiority by adopting a camouflage colouring similar to the substratum (sponges, corals or other) on which they live. The images show two interesting examples of their excellent mimicry capability.

C

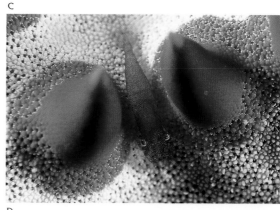

A

D

B - The Emperor prawn (Periclimenes imperator) is typically associated with the large nudibranch known as Spanish dancer (Hexabranchus sanguineus) exploiting the greater capacity to move and the almost total absence of predators of this red mollusc.

C - The large spines at the aboral side of many starfish are an insuperable barrier for predators of these prawns (Periclimenes sp.) if they manage to see them. Camouflage colouring varies from one species to another depending on the substratum.

B

E

F

E - Galatheidae are crustaceans having an abdomen left partially exposed by the shell.
The strange yellow and black species (Allogalathea elegans) lives in association with the crinoid Comanthus bennetti adopting its colouring to perfection.

F - These crustaceans (Dasycaris zanzibarica) of the Pontoniinae subfamily are found only on the long sea whip colonies of black corals of the Cirripathes genus where they live in pairs. Their light and dark yellow stripes are particularly good camouflage when the polyps are expanded.

allows the blenny to approach without hesitation and when it attacks to bite and rip away a piece of skin it is too late to flee. Equally advantageous for the mimic is the imitation of a dangerous species. This occurs in Red Sea blennies of the *Meiacanthus nigrovittatus* and *Ecsenius gravieri* species.

The former is characterized by its large, pointed eyeteeth connected to a poisonous gland, an effective deterrent against all attackers. *Ecsenius gravieri*, on the other hand, is totally devoid of defence and makes up for this weakness by showing the same colouring as the aggressive species.

As has been observed in laboratory studies, predators who have had a negative experience with *Meiacanthus* will not even attempt to eat *Ecsenius*. Another example of fish passing for what they are not is the case of the puffer fish (Tetraodontidae) of the *Canthigaster* genus and file fish (Monacanthidae) of the *Paraluteres* genus.

The former have toxic flesh disdained by predators whereas the latter are, of course, excellent and, moreover, defenceless.

To avoid being eating, the *Paraluteres* have evolved an appearance identical to that of the puffer fish present in their habitat. Thus pairs of fish have developed which are at first sight identical both in movement and markings, e.g. Paraluteres arquat and *Canthigaster margaritata* in the Red Sea or *Paraluteres prionurus* and *Canthigaster valentini* (the best known pair) common in much of the Indo-Pacific. Colours, however, are not only deceiving. On the contrary, they can serve to transmit precise and unmistakable messages. Groupers can rapidly change colour depending on whether they feel attacked, are afraid or are resting. The different colourings accompanying the development and sex change described in the paragraph on reproduction are none other than systems designed to facilitate an encounter between the two sexes. It is not rare for colours to clearly differentiate young fish from

G

H

I

J

G, H - The sequence illustrates the remarkable modifications of a cowrie (Cypraea tigris) in the space of 24 hours. A distinguishing feature of these gastropod molluscs, also called porcelain for their shiny shell, is their large protective mantle. This large lamina-like formation completely envelopes the shell as the mollusc - more active by night - moves amid the corals in search of food. The mantle serves both to protect the shell and to camouflage the creature.

I - Some cypraea are commonly called "allied cowries" as they always live in association with soft corals (Dendronephthya sp.) taking on the same colouring.

J - A cowrie entirely hidden by its mantle. The colour and growths make it similar to a piece of rock with algae or a strange sponge.

C

adults, thus avoiding pointless and harmful combat between members of the same species.

Lastly, a bright colouring, called "aposematic", always warns potential enemies of attacks which could result unwise. This occurs both in invertebrates and in fish. The splendid blue colouring of the *Linckya laevigata*, for this very shade one of the best known and admired beauties of the Pacific, serves, in actual fact, to warn possible predators that its flesh cannot be eaten. Other organisms such as prawns of the Periclimenes genus or small gastropod molluscs *(Thyca sp.)* take advantage of this, living in close contact with it and taking on the same colour. Nudibranchs are often impressively coloured alert predators of the very scarce appeal of their flesh. Aposematic colouring is found in numerous fish, including many puffer fish, boxfish and cobra fish (*Pterois* and *Dendrochirus genera*). In some cases, the accentuated colouring indicates only the dangerous part of a fish as occurs in many of the Acanthuridae in which the spines on the tail peduncle (actually modified scales) are often transformed into sharp blades similar to scalpels.

D

E

A - Although the body of the young boxfish (Canthigaster sp.) is covered with a skin capable of secreting a repellent toxin, they like to hide in corals.

B - Blennies are regularly found in the cavities of reefs, especially those just the same size as their bodies. Once in a safe place, they watch carefully over their territory.

C - The Balistoides conspicillum, *or clown triggerfish, is one of the best known and most colourful species in the Indo-Pacific; it can grow to 50 centimetres in length.*

D, E - The pictures show a Balistapus undulatus *(top) and a* Balistoides viridescens *(bottom). The latter species, known as the titan triggerfish, is particularly aggressive, especially when defending its home.*

F - The messages transmitted by colour often regard the bad taste of the creature exhibiting a particular colouring. This blue starfish of the Pacific, Linckia laevigata, has repellent flesh.

G - The bright, contrasting colouring of the spines of surgeonfish (Naso Lituratus) accentuate these potentially dangerous defensive weapons which divers should also beware of.

H - A giant pufferfish (Arothron stellatus) in a characteristic pose of attack and in normal conditions. This species is one of the largest of the Tetradontidae family and can grow to 90 centimetres in length.

H

I

J

F

G

I, J - The colouring of a fish does not serve merely to hide it. Often it makes it possible to distinguish the young from the adults thus avoiding pointless intraspecific battles. The two photographs show the difference between the adult (top) and young (bottom) of the Emperor angelfish (Pomacanthus imperator).

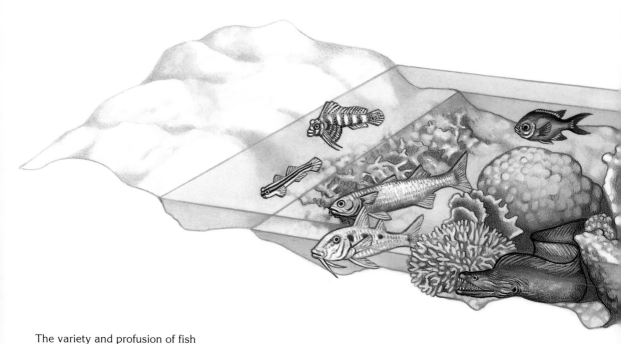

The variety and profusion of fish and organisms living on a reef increase with the complexity of the habitat. The Indo-Malay archipelago hosts approximately 2000 species of fish; more than 1500 live along the Great Barrier Reef; approx. 500 live in the Caribbean; 450 in Hawaii; 700-900 in the islands of the Indian Ocean and almost 800 in the Red Sea, without counting the invertebrates accompanying them.

Such a multitude of species, admirable example of the concept of biodiversity which became famous with the public at large after the summit on the environment in Rio de Janeiro, makes it easy to understand, at least in numerical terms, how 150 species can be found in less than 50 metres of reef and more than 50 around a single coral pinnacle. Nonetheless, no expert, despite all the attempts made, has yet managed to explain in full the wealth of reef life. Only detailed

The zonation of the fish along a reef varies greatly according to the reef and the part considered. The distance from the coast, presence of a lagoon, exposure to winds and to currents are other factors affecting the composition of the species along a horizontal section

stretching towards the open sea. The drawing is to be taken as a synthesis of the many possibilities; more importance has been given to the categories to which the fish belong - and of which they are examples - than to a true taxonomical representation.

a) The innermost sandy band influenced by the tides:
1) Blennies
2) Gobies

b) Lagoon fish:
3) Mullet
4) Goat-fish

c) The lagoon coral band:
5) Pomacentridae
6) Morays

d) The ramified coral band close to the outermost slope of the reef
7) Butterflyfish
8) Labridae
9) Parrotfish
10) Surgeonfish
11) Filefish
12) Pufferfish

e) The outermost slope of the reef and open sea
13) Grunters
14) Squirrelfish
15) Snappers
16) Groupers
17) Carangids
18) Barracudas
19) Sharks

A - The most coloured parts of the body of many sharks (in the photograph a Carcharhinus albimarginatus) help them to recognize each other and perhaps also, as argued by some, to distract their prey.

and prolonged studies could help to reveal what makes it possible, but these discoveries would take years and fill hundreds of pages. There must certainly be an overlapping in the exploitation of the resources and even of space - both in the case of sessile and other invertebrates and fish.
A crevice can host nocturnal fish during the day and offer shelter to daytime ones at night.
Probably the best explanation found until now is that seeing a reef as a mosaic developing not just in the three spatial dimensions but also in time. Were it possible to identify all the fish present, it would emerge that not only do these disappear to be replaced by others in a few months, basically as a result of hunting, but also that the species composition varies on a seasonal or annual basis.
Despite this rapid exchange the reefs, now having reached maturity and temporal stability, present a well organized community, for some ecologists comparable to those of land habitats. This would

A

A - Monacanthidae, better known as filefish for the roughness of their skin, are shy and tend to remain hidden much of the time.

B - A pufferfish (Arothron sp.) shelters behind an umbrella of Acropores.

C - A black spotted pufferfish (Arothron nigropunctatus) emerges from a crevice at the base of a reef.

B

C

suggest that the biodiversity of coral reefs must be ascribed to accurate sharing of the resources, intended in the widest sense of the term. This is obtained mainly through an extreme specialization in the exploitation of the food available. A comparison of the type of prey captured by 7 species of Serranidae and 17 Scorpaenidae, all carnivores and living in the same section of a reef, revealed that each species differed from the others both in period of hunting, size of prey and area in

D - The caves and crevices opening at the base of a reef are an ideal habitat for species that are not great lovers of light or those seeking a safe refuge for rest. Platycephalidae or crocodilefish are not rare in these environments where they remain immobile without burying themselves.

D

which they lived and were hunted. In particular, only one species of Serranidae fed on fish, two captured fish and crustaceans, but each different types whereas the others were practically omnivorous. An equally complex differentiation in feeding requirements was also found in nocturnal squirrel fish; although they fed mainly on crustaceans, they had different hunting grounds and each selected its prey according to size and type (crabs, prawns, etc.). This allowed seven potentially competitive species to cohabit in perfect equilibrium. The concept of living space for reef organisms, as for all living beings, must, however, be extended to the more precise concept of "ecological niche", a term used by ecologists to describe not just the physical space occupied by an organism but also its role within the community and its position with regard to the environmental gradients which in a reef may be exposure to the currents, light intensity, the nature of the

E

F

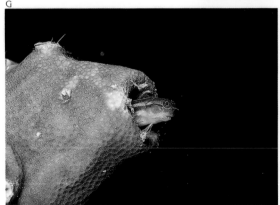

G

H

I

E, F - Nurse sharks (Nebrius ferrugineus) love to hide inside cavities where they remain immobile during the day. By night they are more active and swim close to the sea bottom inspecting it with their barbels and nose ready to suck up any possible prey (fish, crabs, prawns and polyps).

G, H - The presence of blennies can be considered an example of the life cycle of the reef. The dens they occupy are frequently the empty tubes of sessile polychaeta or cavities dug by molluscs or perforating sponges now dead.

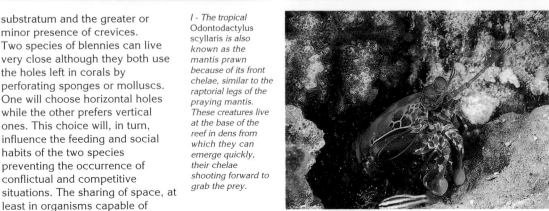

substratum and the greater or minor presence of crevices.
Two species of blennies can live very close although they both use the holes left in corals by perforating sponges or molluscs. One will choose horizontal holes while the other prefers vertical ones. This choice will, in turn, influence the feeding and social habits of the two species preventing the occurrence of conflictual and competitive situations. The sharing of space, at least in organisms capable of

I - The tropical Odontodactylus scyllaris is also known as the mantis prawn because of its front chelae, similar to the raptorial legs of the praying mantis. These creatures live at the base of the reef in dens from which they can emerge quickly, their chelae shooting forward to grab the prey.

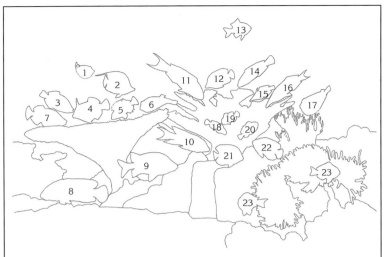

The behaviour of fish living in close contact with or feeding on coral colonies is often directly influenced by coral types.
The drawing compares two imaginary colonies, one umbrella and one ramified, with a number of typical reef fish. As in the previous case, the illustration is to be considered as a general example despite the attention to detail. Its main objective is to stimulate the curiosity of divers and heighten their powers of observation.

1) Canthygaster pygmaea
2) Chaetodon auriga
3) Balistapus undulatus
4) Amanses scopas
5) Cirrhitichthys oxycephalus
6) Arothron sp.
7) Rhynecanthus assasi

8) Cephalopholis sp.
9) Sargocentron spiniferum
10) Epibulus insidiator
11) Thalassoma lunare
12) Chaetodon citrinellus
13) Chromis viridis
14) Stethojulis sp.
15) Oxymonacanthus longirostris
16) Gomphosus caeruleus
17) Arothron hispidus
18) Paragobiodon echinocephalus
19) Gobiodon citrinus
20) Caracanthus sp.
21) Chaetodon sp.
22) Centropyge flavissimus
23) Amphiprion bicinctus

moving, must thus be interpreted in a far broader and less rigid manner than thought.
The confines within which a species moves exceed the space necessary for feeding, reproduction or other activities. Refuges, mere overhangs, fissures and caves, holes left by tube worms or molluscs, or even open spaces close to corals and Gorgonians, are but a part of the space in which fish live and is destined to be occupied for variable periods. It is smaller than the space destined for nutrition, often with well defined characteristics sufficiently familiar to the fish who use them enough to be defined as "dens".
Of course, the division of spacehas a greater importance for those fish which, during the reproductive period, choose specific areas of the sea bed as nests or which are by nature territorial. For these species, too, it is possible to recognize increasingly limited areas each responding to specific requirements: social relations, nutrition, reproduction. Typical cases of this division are found in blennies and in Pomacentridae as well as in the strange "eel garden", Congridae always living fused to the substratum. These fish, one of

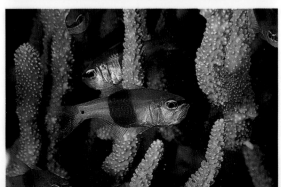

A - Fish and crustaceans can cohabit peacefully, as shown in this particular image.

B - A small threatening crab tries to defend the territory it has appropriated amidst the corals. Its chelae, forward, it faces the diver as if he was a possible enemy.

C - Blackstriped cardinal fish (Archamia zosterophora) live in shoals between ramified corals inside lagoons or in the least exposed parts of reefs.

D

D - The sandy
bottoms found
inside lagoons or at
the base of reefs are
extremely rich in life
although to divers
they appear
uninhabited.
The volcano-like
hills accentuating
the lunar aspect of
the sea bed hide
worms which feed
on the organic
substances present
in the sediment.

the few cases of living sessile
vertebrates, together with conger
eels and moray have an eel-
shaped body kept inside a long
tunnel dug in the sand into which
they plunge like lightning should a
diver or another potential menace
approach. The front part of the
body emerges from the tunnel and
sways as it feeds on plankton
brought by the currents.
Their mutual position is strictly
determined by the fact that not
even during mating, achieved by
interlacing the head and trunk,
do they totally leave their tunnel.
At the end of the larval phase, the
young dig a tunnel at the edge of
the colony thus maintaining its
unity.

E

F

E - Just a hasty
move or one
exaggerated air
bubble and the
plumed corolla of
tentacles of this
sedentary
polychaeta will
vanish in a flash.

F - The gobies of the
Amblyeleotris genus
are typical
inhabitants of sandy
beds or detritus and
live perpetually
close to their dens
into which they are
ready to disappear -
swimming
backwards to avoid
losing sight of the
possible attacker.

G - One of the most
interesting
relationships
between fish and
territory is that
found in the so-
called garden eels
(in the photograph
Heteroconger
hassi).

G

109

Fish living in shoals do not always maintain the same distance from each other. Feeding behaviour, reproductive cycles and the attack of a predator are all events which can - sometimes drastically - modify the form and compactness of a shoal. Often, as seen in these four images, environmental factors alter the nature of the group. The example, fruit of research carried out in the Indian Ocean by British researchers, illustrates the behaviour of Lutjanus monostigma according to the intensity of the current.

1) Phase of slack water. There are practically no currents and the shoal is compact.
2) The current is approximately 1 kilometre/hour. The fish start to widen their distance from each other.
3) The current is approx. 2 km/h. The fish form a row close to the sea bottom, well apart from each other.
4) The current is 3 kilometres/h. The fish group loosely seeking shelter in the corals.

A - Parrotfish are only rarely territorial, they prefer in fact moving towards areas richer of food.

B

B - The rainbow hawkfish (Paracirrhites arcuatus) *generally lives resting on corals, where it finds secure refuge.*

3

4

The Pempheridae, commonly known among divers as glassfish for the transparency and shine of their bodies, have decidedly nocturnal habits. At the top is the daytime behaviour of these fish that remain inside caves in large numbers forming large compact shoals. By night (drawing bottom) the same fish leave their refuge and scatter along the reef walls splitting up into smaller groups busy catching plankton.

Considering the close relationship existing between the sun's rays and corals, it is perhaps not wrong to define coral reefs as daughters of the sun. By day reefs appear particularly rich in life and it is certainly no chance that 70% of coral fish species are typically daytime fish.

What happens when, after sunset, night advances forcing human observers to use a torch to see the forms of live at work?

The species populating the well illuminated reefs and lagoons scatter towards safer areas, often true dens used habitually and that the fishes know how to find, though only if there is sufficient light. Many fish have shown during the day an unquestionable sense of orientation but fail to find their dens in the dark.

Surgeonfish and angelfish plunge deeper in search of narrow cracks to protect their high, compressed bodies; butterflyfish take refuge in the crevices of the corals followed by parrotfish. Many of these rapidly start to secrete the mucous cocoon destined to defend them during the night, acting as a barrier against smells and obstructing the hunting of those nocturnal species, such as moray, which use their sense of smell to track down their prey. *Labridae*, practically ubiquitous during the day, disappear, burying themselves beneath the sediments or concealing themselves inside cracks where, as many other species, they lose their bright colours and take on duller shades characterized by dark bands or patches thus becoming less visible. The countless small fish acting as an entourage to the large Acropores and the other bushy corals hide in the maze of branches to wait for the night to pass. In contrast the caves and the darkest parts of the reefs, during the day sheltering soldier fish, squirrel fish, puffer fish, morays, glass fish, priacanthidae and apogonidae empty, abandoned by that 10% or so of fish considered by experts as typically nocturnal. It is interesting to note how the species with nocturnal habits have evolved, independently one from the other, in response to a common need; the most

A

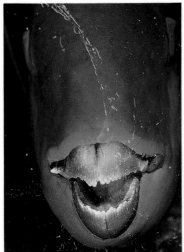

A, D - Parrotfish (Scarus sp.) disappear from the reef during the night. After sunset they move towards deeper waters seeking refuge inside crevices where they remain immobile. Some species drastically change colour taking on more faded and less striking hues to become less visible. Other species secrete a copious mucous enveloping the whole fish in a sort of cocoon. This shield is believed to serve to prevent predators finding the sleeping and defenceless fish by sense of smell.

B - A small black-spotted pufferfish (Arothron nigropunctatus) with its unusual colouring caught at the entrance to the refuge chosen for the day. This species is nocturnal and only tends to come out in the dark.

B

D

C

E

F

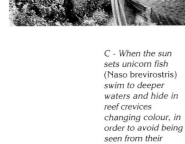

C - When the sun sets unicorn fish (Naso brevirostris) swim to deeper waters and hide in reef crevices changing colour, in order to avoid being seen from their natural predators.

E - Driven by their scarce inclination for well-illuminated waters, blue-striped snappers (Lutjanus kasmira) and white-spotted soldierfish (Myripristis vittata) gather close to or inside nooks. By night these fish scatter to hunt.

F - A shoal of black-spotted grunters (Plectorhinchus gaterinus) in the shade of a reef ledge. This species also has twilight and nocturnal habits and hunts in the dark.

characteristic of these specific adaptations is colouring, often red, and large eyes (adaptations also found in deep sea fish). These fish start to hunt at sunset when the reduction in the light intensity triggers particular mechanisms all over the reef and surrounding waters, from which the large predators arrive. It is, in fact, well known that the alternation of light and darkness influences the movements of plankton; during the day they tend to swim deeper and rise again towards the surface at night. This mass migration, involving millions of tiny beings from many different zoological groups, is responsible for the nocturnal transformation of the reef. The coral polyps expand, soft corals swell their plastic skeletons and Gorgonians flourish. Crinoids settle and expand their arms to intercept the crop of plankton. The tube polychaetes are also more courageous extending their feathery tufts and mobile ophiuroids; crabs and prawns move at night, more confident for the reduction in their

A

B

C

D

E

A - The large eye of the Priacanthus hamrur is a typical example of adaptation to nocturnal life.

B - A shoal of Soldierfish (Myripristis vittata) swims in front of the photographer showing the vivid colours.

C - Sabre squirrelfish (Sargocentron spiniferum) gather by day before caves or in poorly illuminated areas. In the background, in the cave, are a group of soldierfish.

D, E - Squirrelfish embody the most typical characteristics of fish with nocturnal habits: red colouring and large eyes.

potential predators. The sandy sea bottom, by day almost deserted and of little interest, fills with small gobies and sole, starfish and urchins such as the Diadema with its long spines or molluscs which on the sediments leave clearly visible traces of their nocturnal incursions, destined to

F

F, G - The alternation of day and night influences the life of both vertebrates and invertebrates. Soft corals change remarkably in appearance when night descends on the reef. Only then do the Alcyonacea start to expand in the water to increase the chances of nourishment for the polyps. There is such a difference between day and night that some species even double or triple in size.

G

I

H

J

K

H - A large moray (Gymnothorax javanicus) is portrayed in this picture. Morays are among the most formidable of nocturnal predators thanks to a sensitive sense of smell which allows them to track down their prey by following the scent.

I, J - The colonies of corals of the Tubastrea genus are roughly ramified and not very striking during the day but acquire an extraordinary yellow colouring by night when their polyps fully expand their yellow tentacles.

K - A moray (Gymnothorax fimbriatus) surprised hunting at night. During the day it is quite difficult to see these fish swimming; they prefer in fact to stay in their grottoes and to wait for the darkness to go hunting.

DAY

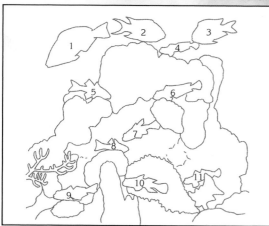

be cancelled rapidly the next day by the tidal currents. The rhythms and movements of the nocturnal animals are often very regular and at times directly influenced by the moon and star light.

Although the number of large nocturnal predators is proportionately reduced compared with the day, the light produced by a full moon is sufficient to limit the movements of the smallest species. These remain decidedly closer to their refuge and form shoals instead of scattering on nights with a full moon.

A

A - Even soft corals, with darkness, change form: they expand polyps looking like delicate flowers.

B - A small but stinging sea anemone (Alicia mirabilis) starts to swell as the night progresses until its column is fully expanded and its tentacles stretched out in the water creating a mortal trap for many small organisms.

C - Driven back by light, the brittle stars or ophiurans leave their refuge by night climbing up on other organisms to reach areas better suited to their search for food.

B

C
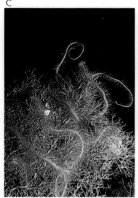

D

Thanks to their complex form, the large coral formations provide numerous places of refuge used by fish according to their needs and habits. In some cases the same refuge is even used alternately by day and by nocturnal fish as it has been cleared up in these two drawings, based on studies carried out in the Caribbean. On the left it is possible to observe the typical situation during the day, on the right you can see the same group of fish during the night.

D - A ghost crab, made darker by the night, moves over the branches of a soft coral seeking tiny invertebrates, detritus and particles of organic matter trapped between the tentacles of the polyps.

1) Sparisoma sp.
2) Chromis cyanea
3) Stegastes partitus
4) Gobiosoma sp.
5) Phaeoptyx pigmentaria
6) Labrisomus sp.
7) Apogon maculatus
8) Apogon townsendi
9) Coryphopterus sp.
10) Coryphopterus glaucofraenum
11) Gobiosoma dilepsis
12) Gymnothorax miliaris

The fish corresponding to no.s 1, 2, 3, 4, 6, 9, 10, 11 are daytime fish. The fish corresponding to numbers 5, 7, 8, 12 are nocturnal.

NIGHT

THREATS TO THE REEFS

Although the scenario of a fierce battle for life, the coral habitat is characterized by a dynamic equilibrium between its inhabitants and the building organisms responsible in thousands of years for reefs of vast extensions, islands and atolls. Obviously, special conditions such as the changes in the level of the sea, bradyseism, volcanic eruptions, typhoons, etc. have from time to time and to varying degrees affected circumscribed points of the reefs, although thanks to their characteristic resilience they have always survived these moments. Today, the situation is rapidly changing for the worse.
The impact of man, mainly because of the increase in population and the social, economical and technological changes caused to the reef ecosystem, has had detrimental effects destined to be repeated too soon for the corals to remedy the situation. In 93 of the 109 countries with coral reefs, on the eve of the year 2000, these have been damaged to varying degrees. This is even more serious as most of this damage has occurred over the last two decades. Among the principal causes for the destruction of many coral habitats is increased sedimentation, i.e. the discharge onto the sea bed and along the coast of large quantities of mud, sand or other inert materials which may remain in suspension for a long period before sedimenting.
As these materials are present naturally in the environment these operations are not perceived in time as a form of pollution.
Corals cannot tolerate excessive sedimentation with the exception of some species belonging to few genera *(Platygyra, Fungia, Acropora, Galaxea, Montastrea)* which manage to survive or dominate in areas suffering from an increase in sedimentable solids. But even these corals cannot resist long against the increase of suspended solids, very often caused by operations of deforestation or territorial

reordering to increase the areas destined for urban settlement, the construction of roads or for agriculture.
The erosion of the soil following the most intense washing away by the rain means that the flowing waters and rivers carry tons of sediment into the sea. This exposes the marine environment, especially the fringing barriers closest to the coast, to damage from events not necessarily occurring in their vicinity.
The farther they are from sources of sedimentation, the more species of corals a reef hosts, the greater the number of colonies per square metre and the greater their growth rates. Coral reefs (see chapter 2) are based on a wonderful symbiosis between polyps and zooxanthellae. An increased turbidness hinders photosynthesis and with it the growth of the calcareous skeletons. At the same time, the polyps are forced to use much of their energy, normally reserved for growth and reproduction, in the production of mucus to banish the particles of

sediment. This reduces their possibilities of defence and competition with regard to the other species such as algae, perforating sponges and molluscs which reduce their wholeness and compactness and increase their vulnerability to the waves.
All together these effects increase the mortality of the corals and reduce the different species, the covering and the dimensions of the colonies.
The sediments prevent new corals from settling, impede reproduction and increase the mortality of larvae during the planktonic life phase. This decline in structural complexity inevitably reduces the number and biomass of coral fish without which a reef's ability to survive is further reduced in an involutional spiral leading to the death of the reef.
The reefs of the Philippines, considered the richest and most diversified in the world, have in many points been devastated by the increased telluric input following deforestation.
Guam, Palawan, Malindi, some

A

B

A - Rivers can become a threat for reefs if the land they cross is cleared to make way for roads, fields or industry. The earth, no longer protected by trees, is eroded by the rain and carried by the river to the sea. Here the sediment will make the water cloud, thus obstructing the life of the zooxanthellae associated with the corals, and may also cover the madrepores of the reefs suffocating them and destroying them for ever.

B - Sediment in suspension carried by the currents can build up on the reefs close to the coast and suffocate them. Without reefs the waves break more violently again removing sediment to cloud the water even more. No one knows where and when a spiral of this kind would end.

stretches of the coasts of Panama, Costa Rica, Barbados, Indonesia and Madagascar are but some of the places where deforestation or even merely the construction of coast roads to facilitate tourism have accelerated the destruction of the reefs and consequently modified the life patterns of some local populations of fishermen. It is not intervention on dry land alone which threatens the corals. The construction of ports and canals usually involves dragging the sea bed. This not only causes a dislocation of the materials on the sea bottom but also its alteration. Digging operations, sometimes even with the use of explosives to open passages in the reef, increase the average depth of the sea drastically modifying the trend of the currents. These will later be deviated by piers and artifical breakwaters which are destined - pardoxically less effectively and at a much higher price - to fulfill the function of the reefs themselves.

In other cases the digging activities serve to extract building materials. Even though this activity has long been practised on a local scale in nations where this is the most easily available or cheapest material, it cannot be forgotten that the need to sustain the new demands for development has led to a tenfold increase in the quantities of material extracted. The airport of Male was built and is being extended using calcareous rock and sand extracted from the closest reefs. In nearby Sri Lanka, in the mid '80s, the material derived from corals amounted annually to more than 45,000 tons. Similar extraction activity normally occurs on many coral islands of the Pacific, in Indonesia, Malaysia, India, in the Comoro Islands and Mauritius. The involutional spiral threatening many coral reefs the world over is also accelerated by all the forms of pollution (tar, plastics, and solid waste are now found along the most isolated beaches of the Indo-Pacific) already affecting the seas of the more industrialized western world and against which the only defence is programmed

development; regrettably, the countries where reefs grow are not always in a position to implement and respect this. If human activities have seriously damaged and in some cases led to the destruction of more than 90% of the coral formations of the Ryukyu islands, despite the fact that Japan has all the resources needed to avoid similar events, it is by no means surprising that the same should occur in economically weaker countries. Unfortunately, there are still many who do not believe that reefs should be treated as a resource comparable with monuments or art treasures and as such in the event of damage economically estimable according to parameters considering the resource destroyed and its use, including its recreative and aesthetic purposes, certainly hard to quantify but of great importance.

The resources offered by reefs go beyond corals alone. There is practically no organism which cannot be exploited.

The populations of the coral world have always exploited the resources of the reefs without changing their equilibrium, often obeying rigid social laws governing time and method of benefit. At present, the increased needs linked to rapid economic growth have also started to influence biological resources. New methods of fishing, more effective and less selective, permit the capture of increasingly smaller fish, preventing the renewal of stocks. This is even more serious when it is considered that the biological cycles of many species are still almost unknown. In many parts of the Caribbean the surface populations of lobsters and other large crustaceans are practically extinct. In the past caught by hand near the water surface, the molluscs of the *Strombus gigas* species can, today, only be fished with the aid of aqualungs, in many cases with rudimental equipment and techniques placing the life of the fisherman at risk. At least two

C

D

C, D - Over-intensive removal of marine life (whatever the purpose) leads not only to the destruction of the single resource but can have serious consequences on the entire coral ecosystem. Our understanding of the relationships between species on a reef is too limited to allow one to be destroyed with impunity. For example Diadema urchins (bottom) and pufferfish (top) are rivals. In the past, when pufferfish were captured in large numbers as souvenirs for tourists, Diadema urchins were able to develop in mass, scraping corals to feed on the algae growing on them, thus causing the destruction of vast coral areas.

species of giant clams *(Tridacna gigas* and *Tridacna derasa)* are virtually extinct in wide areas of the Pacific and many of the species from which mother of pearl is obtained have become so rare as to have forced many nations to promulgate laws for their protection or to limit collection. Many collection shells come from reefs and the rising demand has, in many cases, reduced the density of the single populations.

A

The indiscriminate collection of animal species living on reefs has also been seen to have direct effects both on the reef and on other species; this demonstrates the delicacy of the balance of these ecosystems.
Corals growing in the Red Sea along the Egyptian coast of Hurgada were seriously damaged between 1970 and 1980 by a sudden increase in the population of *Diadema setosum* urchins; in their search for algae on which to feed they also destroyed the coral polyp. Other algae quickly settled on these causing the disgregation of the corals below and attracting large numbers of herbivorous fish.
These drove away the species normally relying on corals for survival. In this way, the excessive proliferation of a single species drastically modified the normal equilibrium of the reef.
Studies conducted following these events have shown that the sudden development of the urchins was due to the excessive fishing of puffer fish *(Arothron hispidus)*, destined to be sold as souvenirs and lampshades and among the

B

C

major predators and natural controllers of urchins. Far better known is the case of the Crown of Thorns *(Acanthaster planci)*, a large starfish bristling with sharp poisonous spines; at night it attacks the corals evaginating its stomach to envelope and digest the soft polyps.
After having eaten, the starfish reabsorbs its stomach and moves away leaving a white patch of dead coral as evidence of its passage. If one considers that in certain areas and periods it is possible to encounter up to 1000 starfish in 20 minutes and in 20 days each one can destroy 15

coral colonies of between 5 and 15 cm, it is easy to understand how the presence of this species has been considered such a scourge as to threaten the survival of reefs. In 1970 one of the most massive invasions against this species ever remembered occurred in vast areas of the Pacific, in particular the Great Barrier Reef.
Although it was obvious that the *Acanthaster planci* had always been present, such an abnormal increase had never been seen. The experts managed to identify one of the probable causes of the increase as the reduction in the numbers of the large gastropod mollusc *Charonia tritonis*, the sea triton, together with favourable environmental conditions.
The triton, although not alone, is the main predator of starfish and its disappearance was yet again to be blamed on man following the intensive collection of this species, much appreciated by collectors.
The dangers threatening the reefs are, however, far more extensive than the examples thus far made may suggest. Some of the most serious are due to changes taking place on a planetary scale.
As many of the biological processes are also chemical reactions, it is no surprise that coral life can be influenced by changes in temperature.
The warming which our planet seems unmistakably to be experiencing has an immediate direct effect on the level of the sea which has increased in the last

A - The Crown of Thorns starfish (Acanthaster planci) feeds on coral polyps. Crawling along the sea bottom it finds its favourite corals and evaginates its stomach onto them, enveloping and digesting them with powerful digestive juices. At the end of the meal a vast area of numerous square centimetres will be completely white and devoid of life.

B - An anchor is firmly fixed to the top of the reef. The monotony of the coral formations, the absence of ramified madrepores and the presence of algae are an indication of suffering on this stretch of barrier. Spectacles and behaviour such as these should be banned. Respect of the ban could be facilitated by providing floating buoys for mooring without the need for an anchor.

century. According to calculations by experts it has been rising at the rhythm of 1-1.2 mm /year.
In some cases, this increase has without doubt favoured the expansion of reefs, but should the rise in the level of the sea increase too quickly because of a more rapid fusion of the polar ices, the corals may not be able to resist this and die. The variations in temperature forecast by many scientists for the future could also modify the climate in the tropical regions, increasing the frequency of rains, hurricanes and typhoons, or the intensity of the waves which would cause even greater destruction on the reefs and, subsequently, the coastal areas fronting them.
The coral islands would, in the end, be submerged, a danger repeatedly stressed by the government of the Maldives, an archipelago with islands rising very few metres above sea level.
Added to this is the frequent occurrence of coral whitening due to a local rise in temperature linked mainly with fluctuations in the surface dynamics of the oceans, increasingly induced by the current El Nino, a current of the southeast Pacific carrying warm waters towards the South American coasts between December and January.
The coral whitening, in turn, is responsible for the initial loss of the symbiont algae.
A prolonged rise in the average summer temperature, even of just 2°C has proven sufficient to cause the coral whitening, whereas a rise of 4°C above the maximum values tolerable for madrepores for a few days caused the death of 90-95% of the corals.
The most superficial parts of the reefs are inevitably exposed to danger resulting from these variations in temperature, which may even be reflected with more serious effects at 10-20 m from the surface, as too UV rays and the decrease in salinity caused by more intense and prolonged rains and to pollution.
The effects provoked by the rise in temperature caused by El Nino in 1982-83 along the reefs of the

D

E

F

C - A totally white stretch of reef stands out among the other perfectly healthy corals. The cause of the death of these corals, the Crown of Thorns starfish, is now far away but active and, perhaps, at work again.

D - The sea triton (Charonia tritonis) is one of the largest gastropod molluscs on coral reefs. Its collection for the beauty of its shell is believed to be one of the causes for the increase in Acanthaster in many stretches of the Great Barrier Reef.

E, F - The sequence shows how the triton follows and attacks the Crown of Thorns, immobilizing it with its strong foot and a viscous secretion before eating it.

eastern Pacific are still visible. It is even believed that the rare fire coral Millepora boschmai, present only in a limited area of Panama, became extinct following these very variations in temperature. Serious whitening was also suffered by many coral formations in Florida, Puerto Rico, Jamaica, Indonesia, Vanuatu, Oman, Thailand, Hawaii, the Maldives and Fiji following the rise in temperature of the oceans in 1987, 1989, 1990 and 1991, this despite the fact that many of these

areas are so far away that in theory they should not suffer the effects of El Nino. Although he problem of coral whitening still presents many enigmas, many think the rise in the temperature of the sea is connected with the greenhouse effect and the increase in the concentration of carbon dioxide in the atmosphere. This is another reason to defend and further study reefs and is the umpteenth demonstration of how their life is linked to that of the planet as a whole.

THE MOST COMMON FISH AND INVERTEBRATES OF THE INDO-PACIFIC AND THE CARIBBEAN

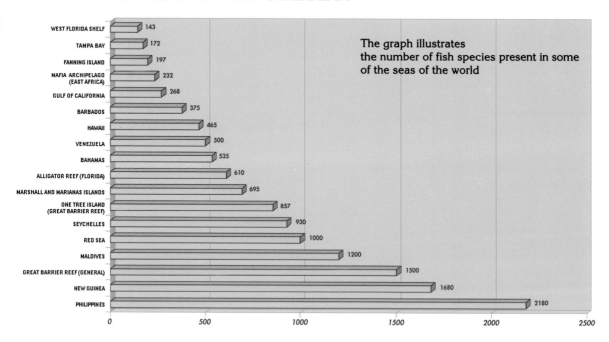

The graph illustrates the number of fish species present in some of the seas of the world

WEST FLORIDA SHELF	143
TAMPA BAY	172
FANNING ISLAND	197
MAFIA ARCHIPELAGO (EAST AFRICA)	232
GULF OF CALIFORNIA	268
BARBADOS	375
HAWAII	465
VENEZUELA	500
BAHAMAS	535
ALLIGATOR REEF (FLORIDA)	610
MARSHALL AND MARIANAS ISLANDS	695
ONE TREE ISLAND (GREAT BARRIER REEF)	857
SEYCHELLES	930
RED SEA	1000
MALDIVES	1200
GREAT BARRIER REEF (GENERAL)	1500
NEW GUINEA	1680
PHILIPPINES	2180

The pages preceding the start of this chapter are an introduction to an ideal picture gallery of more than 300 species of fish and invertebrates. It is by no means a complete list of the thousands of species populating coral reefs. The madrepore formations of the Indo-Pacific alone are inhabited by more than 3000 species of fish and thousands of invertebrates - it would be impossible to describe all in one book. The arduous nature of such a task is even clearer if one considers that the list of beings living in this environment grows year by year.

Many are still to be discovered and new ones can be found even on the reefs most explored by man. The fundamental aim of this last chapter is to describe the basic morphological and biological features of the species most commonly encountered during a sports dive in tropical waters. The bustling community of living beings, of which the diver becomes a part for a few dozen magic moments, seems designed to distract him.

The unskilled eye cannot note the details of the single species, often mixed together, amid the colours, shapes and movements so splendidly illustrated in the pages thus far. Nevertheless, the flight of sea eagles, the passage of a shark or the slow beating of the wings of a large manta swimming before us suffice to make a dive unforgettable and we neglect the rest. We must become familiar with the inhabitants of the reef if it is to be fully appreciated respected and protected.

The clownfish, the triggerfish, the long whiskered mullet, the crocodilefish ever waiting in ambush, the hawkfish, the moray, the damselfish, the coloured labridae and the large parrotfish with their strong jaws, if recognized, can turn a dive into something more than a moment of sport, a sort of stroll among friends.

The photographs show the living organisms in their natural habitat, interacting, feeding, reproducing or defending themselves. Of note in this sense are the photographs of clownfish, voluntary prisoners in their anemones. The drawings make it possible to distinguish the most important features of each species, including those best at camouflage and to find affinities between the various forms of creatures.

Observing the fish illustrated, most in consideration of their importance, it is not difficult to see the affinities existing not merely between highly similar species such as the moray and sharks, but also between damselfish, blennnies, triggerfish, angelfish and butterflyfish.

This will enable the diver or even lovers of nature documentaries not only to recognize the various species but also to distinguish the families and facilitate the search for the precise name of a fish in more specialist and detailed guides.

Whale shark
Rhincodon typus

This is the largest fish in existence and can exceed 12 metres in length. It loves to swim close to the surface feeding on planktonic organisms and small fish. Despite its size it is harmless. Found around the tropics.

Tawny nurse shark
Nebrius ferrugineus

The tapering body of this shark flattens at the belly. The snout is characterized by a pair of side barbels. A nocturnal fish, it prefers to remain on the sea bottom sheltering in caves. It measures 3.2 metres and is found from the Red Sea to Australia.

Ornate wobbegong
Orectolobus ornatus

The flattened body of this fish is suited to life on the sea bottom. The snout and mouth are surrounded by jagged papillae. It lives at depths down to 30 metres. Nocturnal it feeds on fish and invertebrates. It measures up to 2.8 metres and is found from Australia to Japan.

Bambooshark
Chyloscillium sp.

A small shark (75-100 centimetres) and tapered in form, with nocturnal habits and feeding mainly on invertebrates. It tends to remain on the sea bottom at the base of the corals. Found in the Indian Ocean and Australia.

Blacktip reef shark
Carcharinus melanopterus

A coastal water fish recognizable for the black tips of its fins. It prefers lagoons and protected reefs, feeds on small fish and is considered harmless to divers. It can measure up to 1.8 metres and is found from the Red Sea to Hawaii.

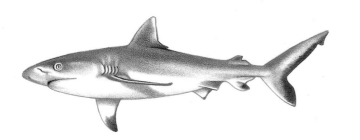

Shortnose blacktail shark
Carcharinus wheleeri

► Very similar to the Grey rock shark, this is distinguished by its colour. The tail has a black edge bordered with white. It has an elongated characteristically rounded snout. It measures up to 2 metres and is found in the Red Sea.

Grey rock shark
Carcharinus amblyrhynchos

A powerful, tapered shark. The rear edge of its tail is black, the tip of its dorsal fin ► white. It feeds on fish and sometimes hunts in shoals. It measures up to 180 centimetres and is found from the Red Sea to Hawaii.

Whitetip reef shark
Triaenodon obesus

◄ The tip of the dorsal and caudal fins are white. During the day it is sometimes seen in caves. Typically present in lagoons and reef channels. It measures up to 2.1 metres and is found from the Red Sea to the coasts of Panama.

Hammerhead shark
Sphyrna lewini

The front edge of the head is undulated. The young tend to form shoals. Not considered aggressive, it feeds on ► fish including other sharks and rays. It measures up to 4.2 metres and is found near the tropics.

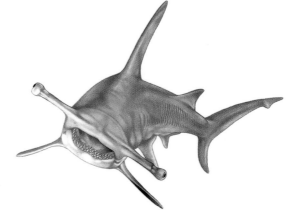

White-spotted guitarfish
Rhynchobatos djiddensis

◄ This shark is flattish with a pointed snout. The mouth is ventral with flat teeth. It prefers sandy bottoms down to 30 metres and feeds on crustaceans and squid. It measures up to 3 metres and is found from the Red Sea to Japan.

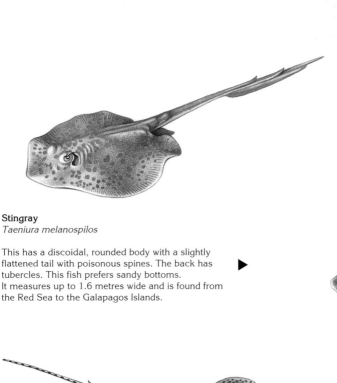

Blue spotted lagoon ray
Taeniura lymma

This fish has a discoidal body of varying lengths, the teeth of the adults being more visible at the centre. The tail has 1-2 poisonous spikes at its base. It measures up to 1 metre across and is found from the Red Sea to Australia.

Stingray
Taeniura melanospilos

This has a discoidal, rounded body with a slightly flattened tail with poisonous spines. The back has tubercles. This fish prefers sandy bottoms. It measures up to 1.6 metres wide and is found from the Red Sea to the Galapagos Islands.

Honeycomb stingray
Himantura uarnak

The discoidal body of this fish is wider than it is long. It favours sandy bottoms amidst corals or close to mangroves. It measures up to 170 centimetres across and is found from the Red Sea to Polynesia.

Spotted eagle ray
Aetobatus narinari

This has a pointed, rounded head with large eyes at the sides. The rhomboid-shaped body has large pointed pectoral fins. It has a very long tail and may be seen in small groups. It measures up to 2.3 metres across and is found near the tropics.

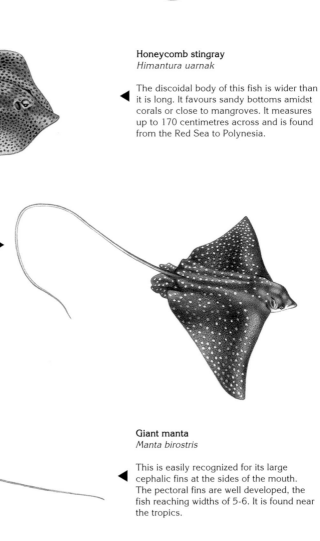

Giant manta
Manta birostris

This is easily recognized for its large cephalic fins at the sides of the mouth. The pectoral fins are well developed, the fish reaching widths of 5-6. It is found near the tropics.

Giant moray
Gymnothorax javanicus

This has a well devoloped, strong body. The snout is short and the mouth wide with pointed teeth.
It prefers shallow lagoons and the outer slope of reefs.
It measures up to 2.4 metres and is found from the Red Sea to Australia. ▶

Leopard moray
Gymnothorax undulatus

◀ A species often found amidst lagoon corals and along the outer slope of reefs. Nocturnal in habits, it feeds on fish and octopus. It measures up to 1.5 metres and is found from the Red Sea to the Great Barrier Reef.

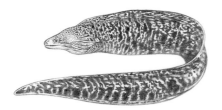

Honeycomb moray
Gymnothorax favaginues

The body of this moray is flattened at the sides and ends with a slightly pointed snout. It feeds mainly on fish and large specimens can be aggressive.
It measures up to 2 metres and is found from Kenya to Papua New Guinea. ▶

Grey moray
Siderea grisea

◀ A small moray with a tapered body, easily recognizable for the black spotted pattern on its head. The young may live in groups. It measures up to 65 centimetres and is found from the Red Sea to Mauritius.

Black spotted garden eel
Heteroconger hassi

This fish is difficult to observe because it is shy and tends to withdraw into its den in the sea bed. Living in large colonies, it measures up to 40 centimetres and is found from the Red Sea to New Caledonia. ▶

Striped eel catfish
Plotosus lineatus

◀ This species has gregarious habits and sometimes forms compact shoals. It has characteristic barbels around its mouth and the back and pectoral fins have strong poisonous spines. It measures up to 32 centimetres and is found from the Red Sea to Australia.

Common lizardfish
Synodus variegatus

Typically found on the sea bed with its eyes partially pointing upwards. It usually remains immobile on the sand waiting for prey. It measures up to 20 centimetres and is found from the Red Sea to Hawaii. ▶

Halfbeak
Hyporhamphus dussumieri

◀ This fish resembles needlefish but is distinguished by the snout terminating in a sort of halfbeak. Living in small shoals inside lagoons, it measures up to 25 centimetres and is found from the Indian Ocean to Australia.

Frogfish
Antennarius coccineus

Well-camouflaged, this fish remains immobile on the sea bottom attracting prey with its long dorsal ray. It lives at shallow depths in lagoons and on outer reefs. It measures up to 12 centimetres and is found from the Red Sea to the American coasts. ▶

Blotcheye soldierfish
Myripristis murdjan

◀ This fish has an oval body covered with large piercing scales. The dorsal fin has strong spinous rays. During the day it often forms shoals in sheltered areas. It measures up to 27 centimetres and is found from te Red Sea to the Great Barrier Reef.

Crown squirrelfish
Sargocentron diadema

Reddish in colour with dark spinous rays on the dorsal fin. Nocturnal in habit, during the day this fish remains in sheltered, poorly illuminated parts of the reef. It measures up to 17 centimetres and is found from the Red Sea to Hawaii. ▶

Sabre squirrelfish
Sargocentron spiniferum

◀ A fish with a pointed snout and well-developed lower jaw. A strong spike starts from the lower edge of the opercula. It has nocturnal and territorial habits. It measures up to 45 centimetres and is found from the Red Sea to Hawaii.

Flashlight fish
Photoblepharon steinitzi

A dark coloured species with very well-developed eyes set above a luminous organ. This can be "lit" or "turned off" by an opaque membrane. It measures up to 10 centimetres and is found in the Red Sea and Comore Islands. ▶

Cornetfish
Fistularia commersonii

This species is unmistakable for the shape of its body and long tail. It is often seen waiting in ambush close to gorgonians or large corals or swimming hidden behind larger fish. It measures up to 1.5 metres and is found from the Red Sea to Panama. ▶

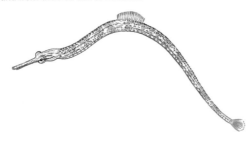

Thorny sea-horse
Hippocampus histrix ▶

Of solitary habits, this fish prefers habitats rich in algae or ramified corals to which it anchors itself with its prehensile tail. It measures up to 15 centimetres and is found from the Red Sea to Hawaii.

Devil scorpionfish
Scorpaenopsis diabolus

Rather well-camouflaged, if threatened this fish will open its brightly coloured pectoral fins. The spinous rays of the dorsal fin are poisonous. It measures up to 30 centimetres and is found from the Red Sea to Hawaii. ▶

Stonefish
Synanceia verrucosa

Practically invisible for its colouring and the shape of its body, this is one of the true dangers of the tropical seas, its spikes being highly poisonous. It measures up to 35 centimetres and is found from the Red Sea to New Caledonia. ▶

Trumpetfish
Aulostomus chinensis

◀ This fish has a compressed elongated body terminating in a tubular snout. The mouth is small with a lower barbel and expands to suck in the prey. It measures up to 80 centimetres and is found from the Indian Ocean to Hawaii.

Schultz's pipefish
Corythoichthys schultzi

◀ This species is often not easily visible because of its camouflage colouring and habits. It remains immobile on corals and gorgonians. It measures up to 15 centimetres and is found from the Red Sea to the Great Barrier Reef.

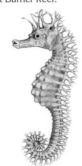

Crocodile fish
Cociella crocodila

The body of this fish is covered with rough scales and the head is flattened. It has a large mouth filled with small, sharp teeth and remains immobile in ambush on the sea bed. It measures up to 70 centimetres and is found from the Indian Ocean to the Philippines.

Leaf scorpionfish
Taenionotus triacanthus

◀ The highly compressed and well-camouflaged body of this fish used sways in the water like a leaf, deceiving prey. It can change its skin periodically. It measures up to 10 centimetres and is found from the Indian Ocean to the Galapagos Islands.

Clearfin turkeyfish
Pterois radiata

◄ This is distinguished from the other turkeyfish for the long rays of its fins and the horizontal white stripes on the tail. It measures up to 24 centimetres and is found from the Red Sea to New Caledonia.

Indian turkeyfish
Pterois miles

The most common of the turkeyfish, this is very similar to the P. volitans of the Pacific. The rays of its fins are poisonous and it can shoot forward to attack. Having twilight and nocturnal habits, it measures up to 40 centimetres and is found from the Red Sea to Sumatra. ►

Scalefin anthias
Pseudanthias squamipinnis

◄ Pseudanthias squammipinnis
One of the best known tropical species this is often seen in large shoals along the walls of outer reefs. The males have one highly developed ray on the dorsal fin. It measures up to 15 centimetres and is found from the Red Sea to Australia.

Yellowtail fairy basslet
Pseudanthias evansi

Similar to the scalefin anthias, this is recognized for the yellow upper half of its body and tail. Forming compact shoals close to the steepest reefs, it measures up to 10 centimetres and is found in the Indian Ocean. ►

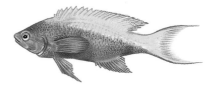

Redmouth grouper
Aethaloperca rogaa

◄ This grouper has a dark coloured compressed body and the mouth is red inside. Often seen inside caves and recesses, sometimes close to the surface. It measures up to 60 centimetres and is found from the Red Sea to the Great Barrier Reef.

Peacock grouper
Cephalopholis argus

This species is present in lagoons and on the outer reefs most rich in madrepore formations. The adults are often seen in pairs. It measures up to 40 centimetres and is found from the Red Sea to Australia. ►

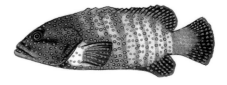

Coral grouper
Cephalopholis miniata

◄ A rather common species and present mainly along the channels crossing reefs and where the water is most transparent. It feeds mainly on fish, measures up to 40 centimetres and is found from the Red Sea to Australia.

Giant grouper
Epinephelus tauvina

This grouper has a tapered body and lives in lagoons and outer reef areas rich in corals. It feeds mainly on fish. It measures up to 75 centimetres and is found from the Red Sea to New Caledonia.

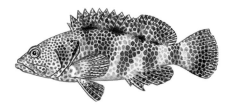

Camouflage Rockcod
Epinephelus polyphekadion

The colouring is fairly characteristic thanks to the dark marbling on the light-coloured upper part of the body. It prefers areas rich in corals and mainly captures crustaceans. It measures up to 75 centimetres and is found from the Red Sea to Australia.

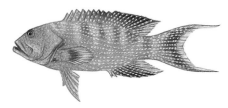

Black-saddle coraltrout
Plectropomus laevis

Close observation shows the strong, prominent canines on its lower jaw. It feeds on fish and remains close to the sea bottom. It measures up to 110 centimetres and is found from the Indian Ocean to New Caledonia.

Potato cod
Epinephelus tukula

This grouper is fairly easy to approach probably because of its size. In some areas where it has become accustomed to accepting food from divers it may be aggressive. It measures up to 2 metres and is found from the Red Sea to Australia.

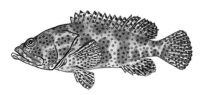

Foursaddle grouper
Epinephelus spilotoceps

This species owes it name to the four dark patches at the base of its dorsal fin. It prefers lagoons and flattish parts of reefs. It measures up to 30 centimetres and is found mainly in the islands of the Indian Ocean.

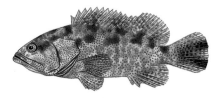

Lunartail grouper
Variola louti

This is one of the most easily recognized groupers both for its bright colouring and the large sickle-shaped caudal fin. It seems most common near coral islands. It measures up to 80 centimetres and is found from the Red Sea to the Marquesas Islands.

Goldstriped soapfish
Grammistes sexlineatus

A shy species tending to remain inside caves and crevices. If threatened its skin can produce a mucous that is toxic for other fish. It measures up to 30 centimetres and is found from the Red Sea to New Caledonia.

Olive dottyback
Pseudochromis fridmani

A gregarious species often seen along the reef fronds
and under madrepore umbrellas from the surface
down to 50-60 centimetres. It measures up to 7
centimetres and is endemic of the Red Sea. ▶

Sunrise dottyback
Pseudochromis flavivertex

◀ A species with a characteristic yellow chrome
colouring on top and blue underneath. It lives alone
or in pairs at the base of coral formations.
It measures up to 7 centimetres and is found from
the Red Sea to the Gulf of Aden.

Longnose hawkfish
Oxycirrhites typus

A species characterized by a long snout and
red/white chequerboard colouring serving to
camouflage the fish when it remains on gorgonians. ▶
It measures up to 13 centimetres and is found from
the Red Sea to Panama.

Pixy hawkfish
Cirrhitichthys oxycephalus

A fish with sedentary habits often seen immobile on
corals where it moves with rapid starts. The larger
◀ males are territorial. It measures up to 9-10
centimetres and is found from the red Sea to
Panama.

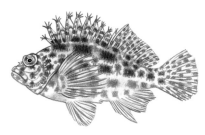

Goldbelly cardinalfish
Apogon aureus

Having twilight and nocturnal habits, this species
hides in groups in caves and recesses during the day. ▶
It feeds on plankton, measures up to 12 centimetres
and is found from the Indian Ocean to New
Caledonia.

Goggle eye
Priacanthus hamrur

◀ A species found fairly frequently close to coral
formations in lagoons and on outer reefs. A nocturnal
fish, by day it stays in groups in poorly illuminated
areas. It measures up to 40 centimetres and is found
from the Red Sea to the Marquesas Islands.

Remora
Echeneis naucrates

A species typically associated with larger fish such as
sharks and mantas to which it adheres transforming ▶
its dorsal fin into a sucker. It measures up to 110
centimetres and is found in all seas.

Bigeye trevally
Caranx sexfasciatus

This lives isolated or in groups, sometimes numbering hundreds of fish, hunting in lagoons and reef channels. It measures up to 95 centimetres and is found from the Red Sea to Central America. ▶

Humpback red snapper
Lutjanus gibbus

A shoal fish, this is frequently seen at the edges of lagoons and along reef channels. It is recognized by its highly arched back, measures up to 50 centimetres and is found from the Red Sea to the Tuamotu Islands. ▶

Mangrove snapper
Lutjanus argentimaculatus

A rather coastal fish and when young most often found close to river mouths. During the day it tends to gather in groups. It measures up to 1.2 metres and is found from the Red Sea to Australia. ▶

Bluefin trevally
Caranx melampygus

◀ A species most easily seen at dawn and sunset when it gathers in small groups to inspect the reefs for prey. It measures up to 1 metres and is found from the Red Sea to Panama.

Small spotted dart
Trachinotus bailloni

◀ Silvery in colour this is recognized by its side spots and long lobes of the caudal fin edged with black. It is typical of lagoons, measures up to 55 centimetres and is found from the Red Sea to Australia.

Two-spot red snapper
Lutjanus bohar

◀ An insatiable predator of fish, living alone but gathering in groups to hunt. Often seen in the largest lagoons and on outer reefs. Its flesh is often poisonous. It measures up to 90 centimetres and is found from the Red Sea to the Tuamotu Islands.

Bluestriped snapper
Lutjanus kasmira

◀ This may form shoals of even a thousand fish gathered around the pinnacles of isolated corals or wrecks. It measures up to 35 centimetres and is found from the Red Sea to Australia.

Yellowfin fusilier
Caesio xanthonota

Having daytime habits, this fish gathers in shoals to
swim close to the flatter parts of reefs or sandy areas.
It measures up to 30 centimetres and is found in the
Indian Ocean.

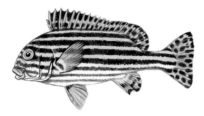

Blackspotted grunter
Plectorhinchus gaterinus

During the day this fish tends to remain in less
illuminated parts of the reef in easily photographed
groups. It measures up to 45 centimetres and is found
from the Red Sea to Mauritius.

Spangled emperor
Lethrinus nebulosus

Frequently seen in small groups on sandy bottoms or
those rich in algae where it may remain in ambush.
It feeds on echinoderms, crustaceans and molluscs.
It measures up to 85 centimetres and is found from
the Red Sea to Australia.

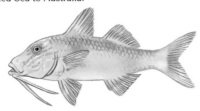

Forsskal goatfish
Parupeneus forsskali

A species typical of sandy bottoms, this is often found
associated with other fish (e.g. Labridae) which
exploit its skill as a hunter of concealed prey. It
measures up to 30 centimetres and is only found in
the Red Sea and the Gulf of Aden.

Suez fusilier
Caesio suevica

A gregarious fish forming large shoals swimming in
surface waters (2-25 metres) away from reefs.
It measures up to 25 centimetres and is only found
in the Red Sea.

Oriental sweetlips
Plectorhinchus orientalis

When young this fish prefers protected areas.
As an adult it is solitary but may form shoals which
allow divers to approach. It measures up to 85
centimetres and is found from the Indian Ocean to
Samoa.

Blackspotted emperor
Lethrinus harak

Solitary or gathering in small groups this fish is most
frequently seen on sandy sea bottoms or those rich
in algae and detritus where it finds invertebrates in
abundance. It measures up to 50 centimetres and is
found from the Red Sea to New Caledonia.

Yellowsaddled goatfish
Parupeneus cyclostomus

Easly recognized by its long barbels serving to
identify its prey, mainly small fish. This is a daytime
fish. It measures up to 50 centimetres and is found
from the Red Sea to Hawaii.

Yellowfinned goatfish
Mulloidichthys vanicolensis

Unlike the other goatfish this regularly forms shoals of perhaps 200 fish by day; at night they scatter to hunt. It measures up to 35-40 centimetres and is found from the Red Sea to Hawaii. ▶

Glass fish
Pempheris vanicolensis

◀ A species with nocturnal habits, this fish tends to remain in compact shoals in caves during the day. It owes its name to the metallic reflections caused by flash light. It measures up to 20 centimetres and is found from the Red Sea to Samoa.

Snubnose rudderfish
Kiphosus cinerascens

This fish prefers sandy areas rich in vegetation and close to the breaker line. By day it lives in groups but these scatter at night. It measures up to 45 centimetres and is found from the Red Sea to Hawaii. ▶

Circular batfish
Platax orbicularis

◀ In adults the snout is concave at eye level. The basic colouring is silvery. The adults live isolated, close to caves or protruding ledges. It measures up to 45 centimetres and is found in the western Pacific.

Pinnate batfish
Platax pinnatus

Similar to *Platax Orbicularis*, this fish is mainly recognized by a black patch close to the anus. It is frequently seen in lagoons, the adults in pairs. It measures up to 60 centimetres and is found from the Red Sea to the Great Barrier Reef. ▶

Teira batfish
Platax teira

◀ The young of this fish prefer lagoon waters. The adults live preferably in pairs although they may form small shoals. The head is rounded. It measures up to 55 centimetres and is found from the Red Sea to New Caledonia.

Black-backed butterflyfish
Chaetodon falcula

This tends to form pairs though it is sometimes seen in small shoals. It will allow a diver to approach fairly easily without fleeing. It measures up to 20 centimetres and is found in the Indian Ocean. ▶

Threadfin butterflyfish
Chaetodon auriga

This lives on mixed coral and sand bottoms where there is an abundance of prey i.e. worms, anemones, polyps and even algae. It measures up to 23 centimetres and is found from the Red Sea to Hawaii. ▶

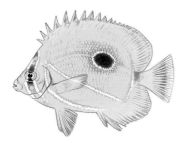

Madagascar butterflyfish
Chaetodon madagascariensis

A fairly common butterflyfish on rocky and coral sea bottoms sometimes those with detritus and at the edges of the outer reef fronds. It feeds on small crustaceans and algae, measures up to 14 centimetres and is found in the Indian Ocean. ▶

Racoon butterflyfish
Chaetodon lunula

This species tends to form shoals during the day. It feeds preferably at night when it preys on nudibranchs, worms and coral polyps. It measures up to 20 centimetres and is found from the Indian Ocean to Hawaii. ▶

Black-backed butterflyfish
Chaetodon melannotus

◀ This is usually solitary or lives in pairs. It feeds on coral and alcyonaria polyps and is therefore often seen among ramified madrepores. It measures up to 15 centimetres and is found from the Red Sea to Samoa.

Bennett's butterflyfish
Chaetodon bennetti

A species living solitary or in pairs. It is seen in lagoons and the outer slopes of reefs rich in corals. ◀ It feeds on madrepore polyps, measures up to 18 centimetres and is found from the Indian Ocean to Australia.

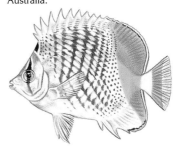

Crowned butterflyfish
Chaetodon paucifasciatus

◀ This lives in pairs or small shoals. It feeds on coral polyps and soft corals, worms, crustaceans and even algae. It covers long distances for food, measures up to 14 centimetres and is found in the Red Sea and in the Gulf of Aden.

Striped butteflyfish
Chaetodon fasciatus

◀ This lives both alone and in pairs. It feeds on coral polyps, small invertebrates and algae. It prefers the flatter parts of reefs, measures up to 22 centimetres and is found in the Red Sea and the Gulf of Aden.

Triangular butterflyfish
Chaetodon triangulum

This species lives only in reef areas where colonies of tabular acropores grow and feeds exclusively on their polyps. It measures up to 15 centimers and is found from Madagascar to Java. ▶

Palefaced butterflyfish
Chaetodon mesoleucos

An uncommon and retiring species, living in pairs in sheltered areas such as wrecks. It measures up to 13 centimetres and is found in the Red Sea (centre-south) and the Gulf of Aden. ▶

Indian butterflyfish
Chaetodon mitratus

A species found at average depths (30-70 metres) and steep walls rich in alcyonaria and black corals. Sometimes present in caves at greater depths. It measures up to 14 centimetres and is found in the Indian Ocean. ▶

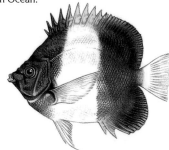

Masked butterflyfish
Chaetodon semilarvatus

◀ This lives in pairs or in shoals. During the day it tends to remain in poorly illuminated areas and under corals. It is more active in the late afternoon. It measures up to 23 centimetres and is only found in the Red Sea and the Gulf of Aden.

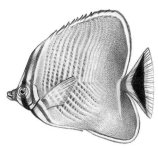

Orange-faced butterflyfish
Chaetodon larvatus

◀ This fish lives alone or in pairs, sometimes close to breaker lines. It would appear to eat only tabular acropore polyps. It measures up to 12 centimetres and is found in the Red Sea and the Gulf of Aden.

Exquisite butterflyfish
Chaetodon austriacus

◀ This prefers the bottoms of lagoons rich in corals and reefs exposed to the waves. It feeds on coral polyps and perhaps also anemones. The young are territorial. It measures up to 13 centimetres and is only found in the Red Sea.

Blackpyramid butterflyfish
Hemitaurichthys zoster

◀ A species with gregarious habits often seen close to the most vertical outer reef walls and in the presence of currents. It feeds on zooplankton, measures up to 16 centimetres and is found in the Indian Ocean.

Longnosed butterflyfish
Forcipiger longirostris

Living isolated or in pairs, this fish prefers the outer sides of reefs rich in corals where it finds invertebrates in abundance capturing them with its long snout. It measures up to 22 centimetres and is found from the Indian Ocean to Hawaii. ▶

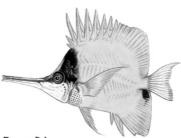

Bannerfish
Heniochus diphreutes

◀ Very similar to the previous species, this is identified mainly by its habit of forming shoals (up to 1000 fish) swimming in the column of water and feeding on plankton. It measures up to 18 centimetres and is found from the Red Sea to Hawaii.

Pennantfish
Heniochus intermedius

A species having variable behaviour, sometimes forming small groups and sometimes living in territorial pairs.It has daytime habits and feeds on zooplankton. It measures up to 18 centimetres and is only found in the Red Sea. ▶

Masked bannerfish
Heniochus monoceros

◀ This fish lives in pairs or small shoals in lagoons and reefs rich in corals. It loves to shelter under colonies of tabular corals or in caves. It measures up to 23 centimetres and is found from the Indian Ocean to the Tonga Islands.

Royal angelfish
Pygoplites diacanthus

Living solitary or in pairs in the lagoons richest in corals and on outer reefs, it often remains in caves or crevices. It feeds on sponges and ascidians, measures up to 25 centimetres and is found from the Red Sea to the Tuamotu Islands. ▶

Emperor angelfish
Pomacanthus imperator

◀ Living isolated or in pairs this fish prefers the lagoon areas richest in corals and reefs with plenty of crevices in which to seek shelter. If disturbed it can emit sounds. It measures up to 40 centimetres and is found from the Red Sea to New Caledonia.

Bluefaced angelfish
Pomacanthus xanthometopon

Generally a solitary fish, it prefers the lagoon areas most rich in corals, channels and reefs with plenty of crevices in which to seek shelter. It is seen between 2 and 25 metres, measures up to 40 centimetres and is found from the Maldives to the Great Barrier Reef. ▶

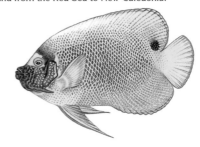

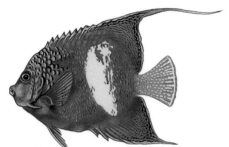

Arabian angelfish
Pomacanthus asfur

Similar to the previous species but distinguished by its larger yellow marking. A solitary fish it prefers sheltered areas and muddy sea beds. It measures up to 40 centimetres and is found from the Red Sea to Zanzibar.

Sergeant scissortail
Abudefduf sexfasciatus

This forms compact shoals in the parts of the reef closest to the surface. It measures up to 17 centimetres and is found from the Red Sea to Japan and Australia.

Clark's anemonefish
Amphiprion clarkii

A common species associated with a dozen or so species of anemones including those mentioned for A. bicinctus. It measures up to 13 centimetres and is found from the Arabian Gulf to the Great Barrier Reef.

Bluegreen chromis
Chromis viridis

A gregarious species typical of coral sea beds and, in particular, areas rich in ramified madrepores around which it forms its territory. It measures up to 9 centimetres and is found from the Red Sea to New Caledonia.

Yellowbar angelfish
Pomacanthus maculosus

This fish prefers coral beds close to the breaker line. It is usually seen alone, measures up to 50 centimetres and is found from the Red Sea to the Gulf of Oman.

Sergeant major
Abudefduf vaigensis

A species common to a number of different of habitats: lagoons, flat beds, reef slopes. It lives in shoals feeding on zooplancton, small invertebrates and algae from the sea bottom. It measures up to 20 centimetres and is found from the Red Sea to Australia.

Twobar anemonefish
Amphiprion bicinctus

Common in the most sheltered parts of the reef and associated with anemones of the species Entacmaea quadricolor, *Heteractis aurora, H. crispa* and Stichodactyla gigantea. It measures up to 14 centimetres and is found from the Red Sea to the Chagos Islands.

Blackfooted clownfish
Amphiprion nigripes

This is found in lagoons and along the outer reef. It is always associated with anemones of the species *Heteractis magnifica*, at depths between 2 and 25 metres. It measures up to 11 centimetres and is found from the Lakshadweep Islands to Sri Lanka.

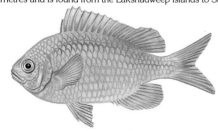

Banded dascyllus
Dascyllus aruanus

A species usually present in large numbers in shallow lagoons and the parts of reefs affected by the tides. It forms shoals around the coral formations, measures up to 8 centimetres and is found from the Red Sea to Australia.

Sulphur damselfish
Pomacentrus sulfureus

Often seen in shallow (1-10 metres) and slightly cloudy waters in the undertow area. It measures up to 11 centimetres and is found from the Red Sea to Mauritius.

Caeruleen damselfish
Pomacentrus caeruleus

This lives solitary or in shoals along the outer slope of reefs close to large masses of corals or detritus. It measures up to 8 centimetres and is found from eastern Africa to the Maldives.

Redbreasted Maori wrasse
Cheilinus fasciatus

This species is fairly common where coral formations are mixed with areas of detritus and sand, feeding on the invertebrates found here. It measures up to 38 centimetres and is found from the Red Sea to New Caledonia.

Half and half chromis
Chromis dimidiata

A gregarious species forming shoals close to reefs, tabular madrepore colonies in particular. It measures up to 9 centimetres and is found from the Red Sea to Thailand.

Domino damselfish
Dascyllus trimaculatus

lThe young of this species live in association with anemones as do the clownfish. The adults gather in small shoals close to corals. It measures up to 14 centimetres and is found from the Red Sea to Australia.

Indian damselfish
Pomacentrus indicus

A species generally gathering in small shoals or living solitary in lagoons or along the outer reef at depths between 1 and 15 metres. The young have an orange spot on the head and back. It measures up to 11 centimetres and is found from the Seychelles to Sri Lanka.

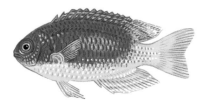

Axlespot hogfish
Bodianus axillaris

This Labridae, solitary in habits, is seen in lagoons and along outer reefs. The young may act as cleaners. It measures up to 20 centimetres and is found from the Red Sea to Australia.

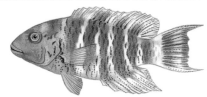

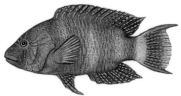

Humphead fish
Cheilinus undulatus

This is the largest known Labridae. Its mouth has large protactile teeth used to suck in the prey. It measures up to 2 metres and is found from the Red Sea to New Caledonia.

Eightline wrasse
Paracheilinus octotaenia

The males of this species form harems of 10-12 females. It prefers mixed sand and coral mass sea bottoms, it measures up to 9 centimetres and is found only in the Red Sea.

African coris
Coris africana

A species present inside lagoons and along the reefs of the undertow area down to 50 metres, on mixed sea beds including sandy ones. It measures up to 38 centimetres and is found in the Red Sea and Indian Ocean. In the Pacific it is replaced by *Coris gaimard*.

Klunzinger's wrasse
Thalassoma klunzingeri

Seen in gradually sloping fringing reefs, this fish often swims in pairs and is easy to approach. It measures up to 20 centimetres and is found only in the Red Sea.

Abudjubbe wrasse
Cheilinus abudjubbe

◀ Present in surface waters in areas where the reef alternates coral formations and stretches of algae. It measures up to 18 centimetres and is found only in the Red Sea.

▶

Broomtail wrasse
Cheilinus lunulatus

◀ The rear edge of the tail of this fish is ragged. Common on gradually sloping fringing reefs rich in corals, it measures up to 50 centimetres and is found from the Red Sea to the coast of Oman.

▶

Yellow tail wrasse
Anampses meleagrides

◀ This species prefers mixed coral sea beds where madrepores, rocks, sand and detritus alternate. It measures up to 22 centimetres and is found from the Red Sea to Australia.

▶

Bird wrasse
Gomphosus caeruleus

◀ This lives in lagoons rich in corals and along reefs down to 30 metres. Its long snout is used to rout out and catch prey amidst corals. It measures up to 28 centimetres and is found from the Red Sea to the Andaman Islands.

▶

Moon wrasse
Thalassoma lunare

The males of this species form harems with some females. Most commonly seen close to the surface, it measures up to 25 centimetres and is found from the Red Sea to New Zealand.

Chequerboard wrasse
Halichoeres hortulanus

The young are often to be seen in the sandy channels between corals. The adults are more common on sandy coral sea beds. By night it buries itself in the sediment. It measures up to 27 centimetres and is found from the Red Sea to the Great Barrier Reef.

Bi-colour parrotfish
Cetoscarus bicolor

The males are territorial and have a harem of females living nearby. It lives at depths beetween 1 and 30 metres, measures up to 80 centimetres and is found from the Red Sea to the Great Barrier Reef.

Rusty parrotfish
Scarus ferrugineus

The males form harems with some females. This species prefers the most sheltered coral slopes from the surface down to approximately 60 metres. It measures up to 40 centimetres and is found from the Red Sea to the Gulf of Aden.

Steephead parrotfish
Scarus gibbus

One of the most active destroyers of corals feeding on their polyps and algae. It is not unusual to see this species in surface waters, its tail protruding from the water as it feeds. It measures up to 70 centimetres and is only found in the Red Sea.

Great barracuda
Sphyraena barracuda

The young form shoals whereas the adults become solitary as time passes. Present in a large variety of habitats close to the coast and in the open sea. It measures up to 1.9 metres and is found in all tropical and subtropical seas.

Cleaner wrasse
Labroides dimidiatus

Typically seen near coral rocks where it tends to remain at the centre of a "cleaning area" waiting for other fish to gather to be cleaned. It measures up to 11 centimetres and is found from the Red Sea to Australia.

Bumphead parrotfish
Bolbometopon muricatum

The young live inside lagoons but the adults, in shoals, prefer the outer slopes of reefs down to 50 metres. Its "horn" can be used to break corals. It measures up to 1.3 metres and is found from the Red Sea to New Caledonia.

Longnosed parrotfish
Hipposcarus harid

Although soliatary individuals are seen frequently, it is not unusual to find numerous fish (up to 500) in groups intent on breaking corals for food. It measures up to 75 centimetres and is found from the Red Sea to Java.

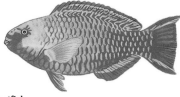

Bluebarred parrotfish
Scarus ghobban

The young tend to feed in groups whereas the adults are solitary. It may live in cloudy waters and can be also seen in subtropical areas. It measures up to 75 centimetres and is found from the Red Sea to Panama.

Bullethead parrotfish
Scarus sordidus

A fairly common species capable of moving considerable distances between its feeding grounds and nocturnal refuges. The young are gregarious. It measures up to 40 centimetres and is found from the Red Sea to Hawaii.

Mimic blenny
Aspidontus taeniatus

It is not easy even for other fish to recognize this blenny. Its most characteristic trait is the downturned mouth. It measures up to 12 centimetres and is found from the Red Sea to Australia.

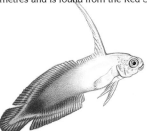

Pinkbar shrimp goby
Amblyeleotris aurora

As is characteristic of the Amblyeleotris genus, this fish lives in a den on the sea bed in symbiosis with a small prawn.
It measures up to 9 centimetres and is found from eastern Africa to the Andaman Islands.

Sailfin tang
Zebrasoma veliferum

This lives almost always alone and only rarely in pairs.
The large dorsal fin is extended only in the event of danger as a threatening signal. It measures up to 40 centimetres and is found from Indonesia to Hawaii.

Convict surgeonfish
Acanthurus triostegus

This is to be seen in lagoons and on predominantly madrepore reefs down to 90 metres. It swims alone or in sometimes large groups (1000 fish) feeding on threadlike algae. It measures up to 26 centimetres and is found from eastern Africa to Panama.

Blackfinned barracuda
Sphyraena qenie

This can always be seen in shoals, the fish swimming very close together near areas rich in currents. It measures up to 1.7 metres and is found from the Red Sea to Panama.

Firefish
Nemateleotris magnifica

A very striking species but not easy to see because it will disappear into its never distant den on the seabottom at the first sign of danger. It measures up to 7 centimetres and is found from the Indian Ocean to Hawaii.

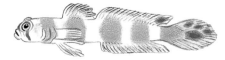

Sixspot goby
Valenciennea sexguttata

Valenciennea sexguttata
A retiring species living in pairs or alone; it digs a den in sandy or muddy sea beds inside lagoons. It measures up to 14 centimetres and is found from the Red Sea to the Great Barrier Reef.

Yellowtail surgeonfish
Zebrasoma xanthurum

During the day this fish swims alone or in pairs. As twilight approaches it gathers in numerous groups to hover above reefs. It measures up to 22 centimetres and is found from the Red Sea to the Arabian Gulf.

Blue surgeonfish
Acanthurus leucosternon

This fish lives in groups, sometimes numbering 30 fish, in calm coastal waters. It feeds mainly on algae, measures up to 23 centimetres and is found from eastern Africa to Indonesia.

Black surgeonfish
Acanthurus nigricauda

This fish prefers lagoons with clear waters and the outer slopes of mainly sandy reefs down to 30 metres. Solitary, it does mix with other surgeonfish. It measures up to 40 centimetres and is found from eastern Africa to the Great Barrier Reef.

Bluelined surgeonfish
Acanthurus lineatus

The territorial and aggressive males form harems with several females. They are common in flatter parts of reefs most exposed to the undertow. It measures up to 38 centimetres and is found from eastern Africa to the Great Barrier Reef.

Sohal surgeonfish
Acanthurus sohal

This fish lives alone forming territories which it defends aggressively. Common on the outer edge of the reef, most exposed to the waves, it measures up to 40 centimetres and is found from the Red Sea to the Gulf of Aden.

Dussumier's surgeonfish
Acanthurus dussumieri

This surgeonfish is generally seen at depths of more than 10 metres (max. 131 metres). It feeds on algae found in the sand and sometimes on rocks. It measures up to 54 centimetres and is found from eastern Africa to Hawaii.

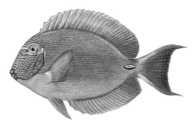

Chocolate surgeonfish
Acanthurus thompsoni

Present on the outer parts and steepest slopes of the reef and along reef fronds. It swims in the column of water in small shoals and feeds on plankton. It measures up to 27 centimetres and is found from eastern Africa to Hawaii.

Brown surgeonfish
Acanthurus nigrofuscus

This species forms large shoals and in this way manages to invade the territory of other surgeonfish and feed on algae. It is seen in lagoons and on the outer reef at depths between 1 and 15 metres. It measures up to 21 centimetres and is found from the Red Sea to Hawaii.

Orangespine unicornfish
Naso lituratus

Seen down to 90 metres on coral beds and on lagoon bottoms with sand or detritus. It feeds on brown leafy algae, measures up to 50 centimetres and is found from the Red Sea to Hawaii.

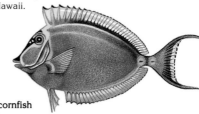

Vlamming's unicornfish
Naso vlammingi

During the day this fish tends to form shoals hovering in the column of water above a reef and feeding on plankton. It can change colour rapidly. It measures up to 70 centimetres and is found from eastern Africa to New Caledonia.

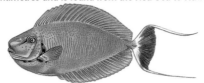

Shortnose unicornfish
Naso unicornis

Often seen in small groups and common in the undertow area or where currents are more intense. It feeds on brown leafy algae. It measures up to 70 centimetres and is found from the Red Sea to Hawaii.

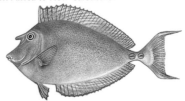

Moorish idol
Zanclus cornutus

This lives in small groups which sometimes join up to form compact shoals. Typical of rocky and coral bottoms it also enters bays. It feeds mainly on sponges, measures up to 16 centimetres and is found from eastern Africa to Hawaii.

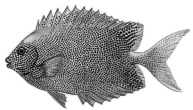

Picasso triggerfish
Rhinecanthus aculeatus

This fish lives in surface waters (1-5 metres) in lagoons and flat reefs with bottoms of sand and detritus. It feeds on invertebrates and small fish. It measures up to 25 centimetres and is found from eastern Africa to Hawaii.

Clown triggerfish
Balistoides conspicillum

Not a common species but perhaps the most striking of the triggerfish. It is solitary and prefers the steepest slopes of reefs full of recesses. It measures up to 50 centimetres and is found from eastern Africa to Samoa.

Blue triggerfish
Pseudobalistes fuscus

This fish prefers bottoms of sand and detritus at the base of the reef. It is less aggressive than other species. It measures up to 55 centimetres and is found from the Red Sea (common) to the Great Barrier Reef (rarer).

Spotted unicornfish
Naso brevirostris

The adults tend to gather in small shoals and swim in the column of water in front of a reef, feeding on plankton. It measures up to 60 centimetres and is found from the Red Sea to Hawaii.

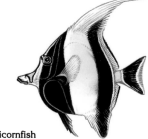

Bluespine unicornfish
Siganus stellatus

The fish of this species are usually to be seen swimming in pairs inside lagoons or on the outer fronts of reefs. It measures up to 40 centimetres and is found from the Red Sea to the Andaman Islands.

Arab Picasso triggerfish
Rhinecanthus assasi

This lives alone in shallow waters on sandy and coral bottoms. The young are common in the flatter parts of reefs. It measures up to 30 centimetres and is found from the Red Sea to the Arab Gulf.

Titan triggerfish
Balistoides viridiscens

A large and rather aggressive fish especially when it is defending its young. The adults live alone or in pairs. It measures up to 75 centimetres and is found from the Red Sea to Australia.

Yellowmargin triggerfish
Pseudobalistes flavimarginatus

This lives solitary or in pairs in sheltered areas or in deep channels down to 50 metres. It makes its bed in sandy bottoms and is not rare close to wrecks. It measures up to 60 centimetres and is found from the Red Sea to the Great Barrier Reef.

Redtoothed triggerfish
Odonus niger

This tends to form shoals above the reef swimming in the column of water to feed on plankton. If threatened it will take refuge in crevices allowing only its tail to protrude. It measures up to 50 centimetres and is found from the Red Sea to the Great Barrier Reef.

Longnosed filefish
Oxymonacanthus longirostris

This is found in lagoons and along the outer edge of the reef down to more than 30 metres. It prefers areas rich in acropore corals and feeds on their polyps. It measures up to 12 centimetres and is found from eastern Africa to the Tonga Islands.

Cube boxfish
Ostracion cubicus

A solitary and shy species preferring lagoons and reefs full of crevices from which it does not stray far. It measures up to 45 centimetres and is found from the Red Sea to New Zealand.

Blackspotted pufferfish
Arothron stellatus

This is the largest of all the pufferfish. The adults may be found in lagoons and along the reef down to 50-60 metres. It feeds on sponges, measures up to 1.2 metres and is found from the Red Sea to New Zealand.

Bleeker's burrfish
Diodon liturosus

A retiring species remaining hidden in caves and recesses during the day. At night it emerges to seek food along the reef. It measures up to 65 centimetres and is found from eastern Africa to Australia.

Orangestriped triggerfish
Balistapus undulatus

The mature males of this species have fewer orange stripes on their nose. It is common in areas rich in corals and feeds on molluscs and echinoderms. It measures up to 30 centimetres and is found from the Red Sea to the Great Barrier Reef.

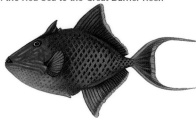

Boomerang triggerfish
Sufflamen bursa

This lives alone or in pairs in areas rich in hiding places. It prefers the outer slope of the reef influenced by the undertow. It measures up to 24 centimetres and is found from eastern Africa to Hawaii.

Harlequin filefish
Oxymonacanthus halli

This is particularly common in parts of the reef where Acropores predominate. This is because it feeds almost exclusively on the polyps of this madrepore. It measures up to 7 centimetres and is only found in the Red Sea.

Pearltoby pufferfish
Canthigaster margaritata

A fairly common pufferfish in fringing reefs and sometimes also in submerged stretches of vegetation. It feeds mainly on algae, measures up to 12 centimetres and is found only in the Red Sea.

Burrfish
Diodon histrix

A nocturnal species this fish remains hidden in crevices during the day. It feeds on gastropods and hermit crabs. It measures up to 90 centimetres and is found in all the tropical seas (Indo-Pacific and Atlantic).

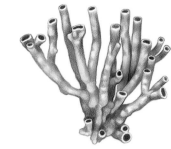

Leucetta chagosensis

A sponge forming globular masses having large apertures containing numerous pores. It grows in less illuminated areas. It measures up to 15 centimetres and is found in the Red Sea.

Tube sponge
Siphonochalina siphonella

Colonies consisting in parallel tubes starting from a common base and ramifying towards the tips. It is not uncommon in illuminated surface habitats. It measures up to 30 centimetres and is found in the Red Sea.

Neptune's cup
Carteriospongia sp.

Sponges in the form of a conical vase tending to develop in shallow waters and sheltered areas. The internal part is finely perforated and full of symbiont algae. It measures up to 50 centimetres and is found in the Indo-Pacific.

Carteriospongia fissurella

An average-sized sponge this is usually seen in the form of a vase fixed to the sea bed by a short, thick peduncle. Inside it is finely perforated. It is brownish or reddish in colour with lighter coloured edges, measures 30-40 centimetres and in found in the Indo-Pacific.

Fire coral
Millepora platyphylla

A fire coral forming laminar-shaped colonies. If observed close up it is seen to be dotted with minute conical formations. It measures up to 60 centimetres and is found in the Indo-Pacific.

Ramified fire coral
Millepora dichotoma

Colonies consisting in flattened branches growing perpendicular to the dominant currents and splitting at the tip. Like all Milleporidae they have a strong sting. It measures up to 1 metre and is found in the Indo-Pacific.

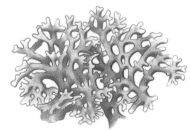

Cerianthid
Pachycerianthus mana

This grows on sandy beds at the base of the reef at depths between 1 and 20 metres. It expands its double crown of tentacles by night to capture small organisms. It measures up to 30 centimetres and is found in the Red Sea.

Yellow green soft-coral
Sarcophyton trocheliophorum

◄ A colonial organism of the Alcyonaria similar to a large anemone are made up of fleshy lobes. It expands rhythmically evaginating the feathered tentacles of the small polyps. It measures up to 25 centimetres and is found in the Indo-Pacific.

Soft coral
Dendronephtya sp.

Ramified alcyonaria capable of expanding considerably at night. The transparent skeleton reveals the coloured spicules. It measures up to 1 metre and is found in the Indo-Pacific. ►

Giant anemone
Stoichacthis

◄ A light coloured anemone with swollen tentacle tips. Amphiprion bicinctus lives in this. It measures up to 50 centimetres and is found in the Indo-Pacific.

Actinodiscus sp.

A colonial organism similar to small anemones although it belongs to a different order (Zooanthidae). It looks like a series of well-opened cups with ondulated edges which tend to close if disturbed. It lives in fairly shallow and well illuminated waters to favour the growth of the symbiont algae and is found in the Indo-Pacific. ►

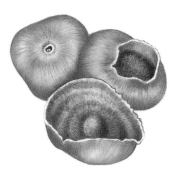

Black coral
Anthipates dichotoma

Colonies made up of sturdy ramifications from which start thinner feathery branches. It prefers poorly illuminated areas, ◄ measures up to 3 metres and is found in the Red Sea.

Spiny row coral
Seriatopora hystrix

Bushy colonies increasingly densely ramified. The branches intersect and end in a point. It measures up to 30 centimetres and is found from the Red Sea to the Great Barrier Reef. ►

Acropora
Acropora sp.

◄ This is the most common genus of the madrepores and the form may vary according to the habitat. Tabular umbrella colonies are typical. It measures up to 2 metres and is found in the Indo-Pacific and the Atlantic.

Leafy coral
Pachyseris sp.

Colonies are usually flattened like leaves. The surface is marked by raised parallel septa. The cups are indistinct. It measures up to 2 metre and is found from the Red Sea to Samoa. ▶

Mushroom coral
Fungia sp. ◀

A madrepore with a characteristic discoidal or oval form with raised radial septa. It is the only coral to be non-colonial and not fixed to the bed. It measures up to 30 centimetres and is found from the Red Sea to the western Pacific.

Madrepora roccia
Porites sp.

Massive colonies having a smooth or only slightly rough surface. The polyps have very short tentacles, often retracted during the day. It measures up to 2 metres and is found in the Indo-Pacific and the Atlantic.

▶

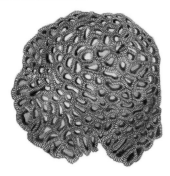

Honeycomb coral
Favites sp.

◀ A madrepore genus with colonies in the form of massive cushions. The corallites are fused to each other with raised walls creating a geometric pattern. It measures up to 60 centimetres and is found in the Indo-Pacific.

Brain coral
Platygyra sp.

A genus of coral producing massive rounded colonies. The surface is marked by raised circumvolute septa. It measures up to 1 metre and is found in the Indo-Pacific.

▶

Rose coral
Lobophyllia sp.

◀ Massive convex or rounded colonies. The corallites form irregular or meandriform lobes. It grows close to the surface, measures up to 2 metre and is found in the Indo-Pacific.

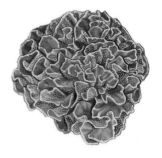

Lettuce coral
Turbinaria sp.

▶

Colonies made up of vertical laminar-like plates folded back on themselves. The surface is dotted with conical growths. It measures up to 60 centimetres and is found in the Indo-Pacific.

Red cave coral
Tubastrea sp.

Ramified colonies with large corallites separate from each other. During the night the polyps expand showing their yellow colouring. It measures up to 50 centimetres and is found in the Indo-Pacific.

Christmas Tree Worm
Spirobranchus giganteus

A common species living in association with corals which cover and protect the tube where the worm lives, only the coloured branchial tuft protruding. It measures up to 7 centimetres and is found in the seas around the tropics.

Fireworm
Hermodice carunculata

A worm with a long flattened body divided into segments. If touched it striaghtens up its many stinging white bristles. It measures up to 35 centimetres and is found in the seas around the tropics and warm temperate waters.

Pseudoceros sp.

Flat worms (Platyhelminthes) are fairly common although not easily seen for their retiring habits. Because of their shape and bright colouring the are sometimes taken for nudibranchs from which they differ for the absence of branchia. They measure up to 5-6 centimetres and are found in the central Indo-Pacific.

Cleaner prawn
Stenopus hispidus

A cleaner prawn with a whitish body and large red cross stripes. It uses long antennae to signal its presence to fish wishing to be cleaned. It measures up to 4 centimetres and is found in the Indo-Pacific.

Hermit crab
Dardanus

A large red crustacean. Not having a complete shell it has to protect itself by living inside large shells. It has nocturnal habits, measures up to 12 centimetres and is found in the Indo-Pacific.

Fiddler crab
Uca inversa

A characteristic crab, the males have a very well-developed left chela. It lives in dens dug close to muddy beaches. It measures up to 4 centimetres and is found in the Red Sea.

Olive chiton
Chiton olivaceus affinis

Chiton olivaceus affinis
A mollusc typical of the tidal area where it lives in crevices, coming out at night. The shell consists in eight plates overlapping like tiles. It measures up to 7 centimetres and is found in the Red Sea.

Cowrie
Cypraea sp.

A well known mollusc mainly thanks to its shiny, oval shell. The well developed mantle covers and hides the whole shell. Measurements vary from one species to another and it is found in tropical and temperate seas.

Textile cone
Conus textile

A carnivorous mollusc with a conical characteristically coloured shell. It lives on sandy beds and hunts by night using poisoned darts dangerous also to man. It measures up to 12 centimetres and is found in the Indo-Pacific.

Ribed tun
Tonna sp.

This large mollusc has a spherical shell decorated with wide flattened ribbing. Despite its appearance the shell is fragile.It lives on beds with both sand and detritus. It measures up to 30 centimetres and is found in the Indo-Pacific.

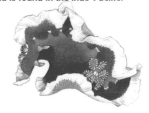

Chromodoris quadricolor

A nudibranch with a bight colouring and tuft formed of fringed tentacles. It feeds on sponges scraped from the bottom, measures up to 5 centimetres and is found in the Indo-Pacific.

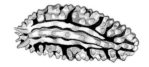

Trochid
Trochus sp.

An easily recognized gastropod mollusc for its strong cone-shaped shell. The outer surface, marked by a raised spiralling line, is often encrusted. It is used for mother-of pearl, measures up to 10 centiemters and is found in the Indo-Pacific.

Egg cowry
Ovula ovum

A mollusc with a porcelain-like shell covered and protected by a black mantle with small scattered spots. It feeds on soft corals, measures up to 10 centimetres and is found in the Indo-Pacific.

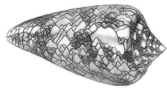

Sea triton
Charonia tritonis

This large mollusc has a spiral pointed shell with a large oval opening. A carnivore, it feeds mainly on echinoderms including the Crown of Thorns starfish. It measures up to 40 centimetres and is found in the Indo-Pacific.

Spanish dancer
Hexabranchus sanguineus

An unmistakable nudibranch for its bright colouring, often fiery red, and the fact that its large mantle allows it to swim. It measures up to 40 centimetres and is found in the Indo-Pacific.

Phyllidia varicosa

A nudibranch with a striking colouring of light and dark stripes. The back is dotted with characteristic conical protuberances. It feeds on sponges and is found in the Red Sea.

Nembrotha rutilans

This nudibranch has a subcylindrical body with developed front rhinophores and a central branchial tuft. It feeds on ascidians. It measures 10 centimetres and is found in the western Pacific.

Chromodoris sp.

An average-sized nudibranch with a sturdy foot used to drag over corals. The colouring is light with a regular geometrical design. It measures up to 5 centimetres and is found in the western Pacific.

Pycnodonta hyotis

A bivalve mollusc similar to a large oyster; the valves are decorated externally with long tubular spines and a zig-zag edge. It measures up to 30 centimetres and is found in the Indian Ocean and western Pacific.

Giant clam
Tridacna maxima

One of the best known organisms of tropical reefs where it lives wedged between corals. The mantle is very colourful with siphon openings. It measures up to 40 centimetres and is found in the Indo-Pacific.

Cuttle fish
Sepia latimanus

The body of this tropical cuttle-fish has numerous growths, tubercles and tentacles with swollen edges. It measures up to 50 centimetres and is found in the central Pacific and the Great Barrier Reef.

Nautilus
Nautilus pompilius
A closely spiralled shell with flame patterns on the top. This has approximately 90 tentacles, measures up to 20 centimetres and is found from the Andaman Islands to Samoa.

Ringed octopus
Hapalochlaena lunulata

A particularly striking species for its yellow and blue stripes. This colouring makes it possible to identify this species and avoid it as it is extremely poisonous and dangerous. It measures up to 15 centimetres and is found from Japan to Australia.

Feather star
Lamprometra sp.

A crinoid with approximately 20 arms, feathery in appearance and of equal length. It has nocturnal habits, hiding during the day in crevices in the reef. Often seen on fire corals, it measures up to 15 centimetres and is found in the Red Sea.

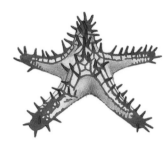

Protoreaster linckii

A sturdy starfish with five triangular section arms. The upper part has numerous well-developed protuberances. It measures up to 25 centimetres and is found from the Indian Ocean to Australia.

Blue starfish
Linckia laevigata

The massive, globular body almost hides the arms when observed from above. It feeds on algae and invertebrates. It measures up to 25 centimetres and is found in the western Pacific.

Crown of thorns starfish
Acanthaster plancii

This is the notorious coral eater. Its arms and body are protected by sturdy poisonous spikes capable of producing painful injuries. It measures up to 40 centimetres and is found from the Red Sea to the eastern Pacific.

Pincushion starfish
Culcita novaeguineae

The massive, globular body almost hides the arms when observed from above. It feeds on algae and invertebrates. It measures up to 25 centimetres and is found in the western Pacific.

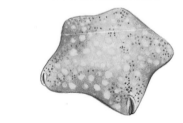

Pincushion starfish
Choriaster granulosus

A starfish with stumpy, rounded arms terminating with a small evagination. It has polygonal, rigid plates on its back. It measures up to 25 centimetres and is found from the Red Sea to the Indian Ocean.

Starfish
Fromia sp.

A starfish with a rigid skeleton; this facilitates breakage and it is often seen with shorter or missing arms. It measures up to 10 centimetres and is found from the Red Sea to Australia.

Sand dollar
Clypeaster humilis

A flattened sea urchin with a discoidal shape and the body covered with very short spikes. It has a 5 petal pattern on the back and tends to bury itself on sandy bottoms. It measures up to 6 centimetres and is found in the Red Sea.

Pincushion urchin
Astenosoma varium

This urchin is identified by its white globular swellings enveloping shorter spikes filled with a toxic liquid. It is dangerous to touch it. It measures up to 15 centimetres and is found from the Red Sea to the Philippines.

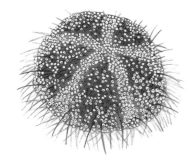

Pencil sea-urchin
Heterocentrotus trigonarius

A pencil urchin with needles becoming gradually thinner close to the tip, unlike the other pencil urchin *H. mammillatus*. It measures up to 25 centimetres and is found in the Red Sea.

Long spined sea-urchin
Diadema setosum

This species is particularly visible at night, remaining hidden during the day in less illuminated areas. It measures up to 30 centimetres and is found from the Red Sea to the Pacific.

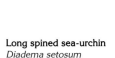

Graeffe's holothurian
Boadschia graeffei

The front end is surrounded by black tentacles, swollen and sticky to capture the detritus it feeds on. It measures up to 30 centimetres and is found from the Red Sea to Australia.

Giant ascidia
Policarpa sp.

A solitary ascidian with very apparent syphons - especially the inhaling one - in a contrasting colour. It measures up to 25 centimetres and is found from the Red Sea to Australia.

FISH AND INVERTEBRATES OF THE CARIBBEAN

Southern stingray
Dasyatis americana

This fish has a discoidal body with pointed snout and wing tips. The tail has 1-2 poisonous spikes at the base. It buries itself in beds, measures up to 1.5 metres wide and is found from New Jersey to Brazil.

Green moray
Gymnothorax funebris

During the day this fish remains hidden in reef crevices where it is easily approached. It may attack if hassled. At night it emerges to hunt. It measures up to 2.3 metres and is found from Florida to Brazil.

Purplemouth moray
Gymnothorax vicinus

This is identified by its yellow eyes and dorsal fin edged with black. It prefers shallow waters and reefs with sandy areas. It measures up to 1.2 metres and is found from Florida to Brazil and the Canaries.

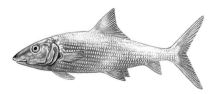

Tiger shark
Galeocerdo cuvieri

An extremely dangerous species capable of penetrating even shallow waters. It is seen along outer reef slopes and reefs away from the coast. It measures up to 5.5 metres and is found in all the seas around the tropics.

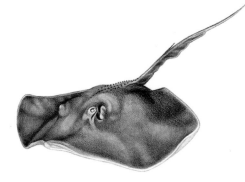

Yellow stingray
Urolophus jamaicensis

The snout and tips of the wings are rounded and its stocky tail has poisonous spikes at the tip. It buries itself in sandy beds close to the reef. It measures up to 76 centimetres wide and is found from North Carolina to Venezuela.

Spotted moray
Gymnothorax moringa

Common in shallow waters, during the day it remains hidden in the reef crevices only allowing the head to protrude. It hunts by night, measures up to 1.2 metres and is found from south Carolina to Brazil.

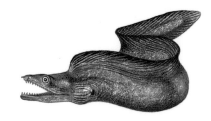

Bonefish
Albula vulpes

This tends to approach sandy coastal beds with the tide. It is seen on coral beds rich in sandy areas and in reef channels. It measures up to 1 metre and is found from New Brunswick to Brazil.

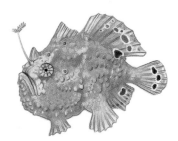

Longlure frogfish
Antennarius multiocellatus

This species changes colour rapidly becoming darker when disturbed. Well-camouflaged it remains immobile until the diver comes too close. It measures up to 14 centimetres and is found from Florida to the Caribbean.

Ocellated frogfish
Antennarius ocellatus

This is recognized by its three ocellate marks: two at the sides of the body and one on the tail. It is seen in rocky and coral habitats at depths between 1 and 150 metres. It measures up to 38 centimetres and is found from north of Bermuda to Venezuela.

Spotted batfish
Ogcocephalus radiatus

This fish has a highly unusual shape, similar to a flattened disc from which the pectoral fins and tail start. It waits immobile in ambush on the sea bed. It measures up to 38 centimetres and is found in Florida and the Bahamas.

Longspine squirrelfish
Holocentrus rufus

During the day this fish remains hidden in reef crevices. At night it leaves to hunt molluscs, crustaceans and starfish. Its spikes can injure. It measures up to 28 centimetres and is found from Bermuda to Venezuela.

Squirrelfish
Holocentrus ascensionis

This remains hidden during the day in the less illuminated parts of the reef close to the bottom and can be approached without difficulty. It has sharp spikes, measures up to 30 centimetres and is found from North Carolina to Brazil.

Blackbar soldierfish
Myripristis jacobus

More common on external reefs, during the day it stays inside caves looking out to obseve divers. It measures up to 20 centimetres and is found from Georgia to Brazil and the Cape Verde Islands.

Bluespotted cornetfish
Fistularia tabacaria

This is seen close to submerged stretches of vegetation and in reefs broken up by sandy beds. It lives alone or in small groups. Sometimes it will allow divers to approach. It measures up to 1.8 metres and is found from Nova Scotia to Brazil.

Lined sea-horse
Hippocampus erectus

Typically associated with the areas abounding in underwater vegetation where it camouflages itself by remaining immobile anchored to the algae by its prehensile tail. It measures up to 17 centimetres and is found from Nova Scotia to Argentina.

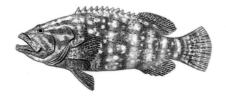

Red grouper
Epinephelus morio

This fish prefers rocky beds and the deepest reefs. It often remains immobile resting on the sea bed for camouflage. t measures up to 90 centimetres and is found from Massachusetts to Brazil.

Coney
Cephalopholis fulva

A gregarious species preferring reefs full of crevices, never straying far from them. It will allow divers to approach but slowly. It measures up to 40 centimetres and is found from Florida to Brazil.

Butter Hamlet
Hypoplectrus unicolor

This prefers coral reefs where it swims close to the bottom. It can be approached but slowly. It measures up to 13 centimetres and is found from Florida (common) to Brazil.

Trumpetfish
Aulostomus maculatus

◀ This lives close to reefs where it changes colour and takes up a vertical position, head down, for camouflage. It is not easy to approach. It measures up to 1 metre and is found from Florida to Brazil.

▶

Jewfish
Epinephelus itajara

◀ This is the largest of the Atlantic groupers. It remains hidden in caves or wrecks and for its sheer size can be dangerous. It measures up to 2.4 metres (300-400 kg) and is found from Florida to Brazil and from Senegal to the Congo.

▶

Nassau grouper
Epinephelus striatus

◀ Common on coral beds where it nearly always remains close to its den. It changes colour rapidly if frightened or curious. Thousands of these fish gather in small areas for reproduction. It measures up to 1.2 metres and is found from North Carolina to Brazil.

▶

Greater soapfish
Rypticus saponaceus

This fish lives in shallow waters close to reefs or on sandy beds. If frightened it secretes a mucous toxic to other fish. It measures ◀ up to 33 centimetres and is found from Florida to the eastern Atlantic.

▶

Barred Hamlet
Hypoplectrus puella

This fish lives on shallow rocky beds and coral reefs at depths between 20 and 23 metres. It is always ready to dive into a crevice but will allow a diver to approach slowly. It measures up to 13 centimetres and is found from Florida to the Caribbean (common).

Indigo Hamlet
Hypoplectrus indigo

This is easily identified by it white and blue stripes. It prefers coral beds at depths between 10 and 45 metres. As the other species it will allow a diver to approach slowly. It measures up to 13 centimetres and is found from Florida to Belize. Common in the Cayman Islands.

Tobaccofish
Serranus tabacarius

This is found close to the bottom where coral reefs mix with detritus and sand. At considerable depths (50-70 metres) it becomes gragarious. It measures up to 18 centimetres and is found from Florida to Brazil.

Peppermint bass
Liopropoma rubre

This tends to remain hidden in crevices and caves and for this reason, although common, it is not easily seen. It measures up to 8 centimetres and is found from Florida to Venezuela.

Fairy basslet
Gramma loreto

This fish is unmistakable for its yellow and violet markings. It lives in small groups in caves or recesses where it is often seen swimming upside down. It measures up to 8 centimetres and is found from Bermuda to Venezuela.

Crevalle Jack
Caranx hippos

The young are gregarious whereas the adults tend to be solitary. Most frequently seen in open water and along the outer front of a reef. It measures up to 1 metres and is found from Nova Scotia to Uruguay and in the eastern Atlantic.

Bar jack
Carangoides ruber

This swims in shoals of varying sizes. Often it joins with mullet and sting-rays to feed on prey found by other fish. It measures up to 60 centimetres and is found from New Jersey to Venezuela.

Rainbow fish
Elagatis bipinnulata

Often seen in open waters and on the outer fronts of reefs. It lives in shoals and seems to be attracted by divers' bubbles. It measures up to 1.2 metres and is found in all seas around the tropics.

Yellow tail snapper
Ocyurus chrysurus

 This fish swims alone or in small groups above reefs. It is more active by night when it hunts fish and crustaceans. It measures up to 75 centimetres and is found from Massachusetts to Brazil.

Mutton snapper
Lutjanus analis

This fish generally prefers sandy bottoms but it can be seen close to reefs and expanses swimming close to the bottom. It measures up to 75 centimetres and is found from Massachusetts to Brazil.

▶

Cubera snapper
Lutjanus cyanopterus

◀ This fish prefers rocky or coral beds at depths between 20 and 55 metres The young are coastal. It is the largest snapper in the Atlantic, measuring up to 1.6 metres, and is found from New Jersey to Brazil.

Porkfish
Anisotremus virginicus

This fish swims alone or in small groups, more numerous during the day. The young act as cleaner fish. It can measure up to 40 centimetres and is found from Florida to Brazil.

▶

Blue striped grunt
Haemulon sciurus

◀ This is often found close to reefs and the reef fronds down to 20 metres where they gather in shoals. It will not generally allow a diver to approach. It measures up to 45 centimetres and is found from South Carolina to Brazil.

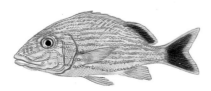

French grunt
Haemulon flavolineatus

This prefers coral beds where it can be seen in shoals sometimes numbering thousands of fish. It is not unusual to see this fish immobile in poorly illuminated areas. It measures up to 30 centimetres and is found from South Carolina to Brazil.

▶

Reef croaker
Odontoscion dentex

◀ This fish prefers rocky areas and shallow coral reefs. It gathers in groups hidden in caves and apertures. It measures 25 centimetres and is found from Florida to Brazil.

Jack Knife fish
Equetus lanceolatus

This fish prefers the less illuminated parts of the reef, remaining in the shade of corals or at entrances to caves. It comes out at night to hunt. It measures up to 25 centimetres and is found from South Carolina to Brazil.

▶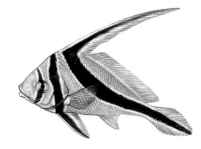

Bermuda chub
Kiphosus sectarix

This fish generally lives in shoals on coral or rocky beds feeding on algae. It measures up to 76 centimetres and is found from Massachusetts to Brazil.

Spotted goatfish
Pseudopeneus maculatus

Often gathering in groups of 4-6 fish, when it hunts it changes colour and the side spots become very marked. It measures up to 28 centimetres and is found from Florida to Brazil.

Foureye butterflyfish
Chaetodon capistratus

This is the most common butterflyfish in the Caribbean. It often swims in pairs close to coral pinnacles. It measures up to 15 centimetres and is found from New England to Panama.

Spotfin butterflyfish
Chaetodon ocellatus

This is seen on coral bottoms or rocky ones in the absence of corals. It generally swims in pairs and at night dark stripes appear on the body as camouflage. It measures up to 20 centimetres and is found from Massachusetts to Brazil.

High-hat
Pareques acuminatus

This fish prefers clear waters and rocky or coral beds. It lives in sheltered or poorly illuminated areas in pairs or in small groups. It measures up to 23 centimetres and is found from South Carolina to Brazil.

Yellow goatfish
Mulloidichthys martinicus

A light-coloured goatfish with a distinct horizontal yellow line on the sides and a tail of the same colour. If frightened it may become darker. It forms small groups on sandy beds close to reefs and allows divers to approach. It measures up to 40 centimetres and is found from the Caribbean to Cape Verde.

Atlantic spadefish
Chaetodipterus faber

This gathers in small shoals swimming in open waters close to reefs, jetties and wrecks. It will approach divers, measures up to 90 centimetres and is found from Massachusetts to Brazil.

Reef butterflyfish
Chaetodon sedentarius

This fish prefers rocky and coral beds at depths between 5 and 92 metres. The young live at shallower depths. It tends to swim in pairs, measures up to 15 centimetres and is found from North Carolina to Brazil.

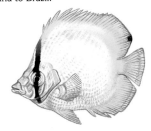

Longsnout butterflyfish
Chaetodon aculeatus

This is a solitary fish preferring the deepest parts of the reef (generally below 30 metres). It often hunts in caves or crevices. It measures up to 10 centimetres and is found from Florida to Venezuela.

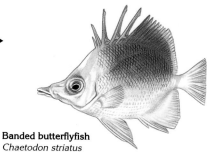

Banded butterflyfish
Chaetodon striatus

This is seen swimming alone or in pairs close to corals, feeding on their polyps though it will not overlook worms and crustaceans. It measures up to 16 centimetres and is found from Massachusetts to Brazil.

Grey angelfish
Pomacanthus arcuatus

This is the largest angelfish in the region. It lives alone or in pairs down to 30 metres in the areas richest in corals. It is omnivorous and will approach divers. It measures up to 50 centimetres and is found from Bermuda to Brazil.

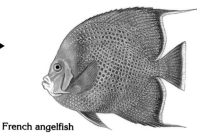

French angelfish
Pomacanthus paru

This fish prefers the most superficial parts of reefs although it may go down to 100 metres. It generally swims in pairs often stopping close to gorgonians. It measures up to 30 centimetres and is found from Florida to Brazil.

Rock beauty
Holacanthus tricolor

A territorial species it never abandons its territory, defending it against all attacks. If approached it will swim away then return slowly. It measures up to 20 centimetres and is found from Georgia to Brazil.

Blue angelfish
Holacanthus bermudensis

This is especially common in the Florida Keys area and feeds mainly on sponges. It measures up to 38 centimetres and is found from Florida to Yucatan.

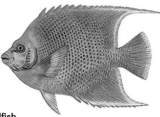

Queen angelfish
Holacanthus ciliaris

This is often seen on coral reefs from the surface down to 70 metres. It will allow divers to approach fairly easily. It feeds on sponges and the young act as cleaners. It measures up to 45 centimetres and is found from Bermuda to Brazil

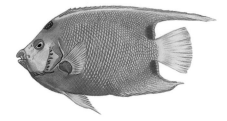

Cherubfish
Centropyge argi

This fish prefers the deepest reefs and is not often seen above 30 metres. It swims quickly in and out of crevices, measures up to 8 centimetres and is found from Bermuda to Venezuela.

Beaugregory
Stegastes leucostictos

A territorial, though not very aggressive, species preferring bottoms of sand or detritus with algae at depths between 1 and 5 metres. It will not flee if approached, measures up to 10 centimetres and is found from Maine to Brazil.

Spanish hogfish
Bodianus rufus

This fish swims incessantly close to coral bottoms with the characteristic jerky movement of the Labridae. It will allow divers to approach, measures up to 40 centimetres and is found from Florida to Brazil.

Hogfish
Lachnolaimus maximus

This Labridae is easily identified by the very elongated three rays of the dorsal fin. It is not rare on sandy bottoms where it digs in search of prey. It measures up to 90 centimetres and is found from North Carolina to Brazil.

Puddingwife
Halichoeres radiatus

Not often seen and difficult to approach for its rapid swimming and suspicous attitude. The young live at shallower depths than the adults. It measures up to 50 centimetres and is found from North Carolina to Brazil.

Blue chromis
Chromis cyanea

 This is common in the column of water above the reef where it forms large shoals of fish intent on eating plankton. It measures up to 13 centimetres and is found from Florida to Venezuela.

Yellowtail damselfish
Microspatodon chrysurus

The young remain preferably between the branches of fire corals and act as cleaners. The adults are territorial but not aggressive. It measures up to 21 centimetres and is found from Florida to Venezuela.

Spotfin hogfish
Bodianus pulchellus

More commonly seen on coral reefs below 20 metres. The young act as cleaner fish. It measures up to 15 centimetres and is found from Florida to Brazil.

Bluehead wrasse
Thalassoma bifasciatum

This is common in a wide variety of habitats: expanses, rocky bottoms, detritus and coral beds. The young, yellow in colour, act as cleaner fish. It measures up to 18 centimetres and is found from Florida to Venezuela.

Queen parrotfish
Scarus vetula

This is seen on coral reefs at depths between 3 and 25 metres where it feeds on the algae scraped off corals. It is not easy to approach. It measures up to 60 centimetres and is found from Florida to Argentina.

Yellowhead jawfish
Opistognathus aurifrons

This lives in dens at the base of corals on sand and detritus. It remains vertical close to the entrance, ready to hide swimming backwards in the event of danger. It measures up to 40 centimetres and is found from Florida to Venezuela.

Doctorfish
Acanthurus chirurgus

This lives alone or in small groups, often associating with other surgeonfish. It is often seen head down nibbling on algae. It measures up to 25 centimetres and is found from Massachusetts to Brazil.

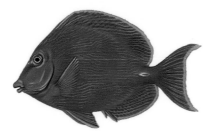

Ocean surgeonfish
Acanthurus bahianus

This fish prefers flat or very slightly sloping reefs at depths between 3 and 20 metres. It often associates with A. Chirurgis. It measures up to 35 centimetres and is found from Massachusetts to Brazil.

Blue parrotfish
Scarus coeruleus

This feeds mainly on algae and for this reason moves actively on the reef stopping to scrape the corals with its beak. It forms large shoals in the reproduction period. It measures up to 90 centimetres and is found from Maryland to Brazil.

Spotlight parrotfish
Sparisoma viride

A species fairly frequent in the parts of the reef where the corals are separated by expanses of algae and marine plants. It measures up to 50 centimetres and is found from Florida to Brazil.

Neon goby
Gobiosoma oceanops

This cleaner fish gathers with others in specific areas where the other fish stop to be cleaned. It measures up to 5 centimetres and is found from Florida to Honduras.

Blue tang
Acanthurus coeruleus

This solitary fish may unite in compact shoals, mixing with other surgeonfish and remaining in surface waters in search of algae. It can change colour quickly, measures up to 23 centimetres and is found from Bermuda to Brazil.

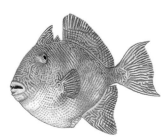

Grey triggerfish
Balistes capriscus

◀ Solitary or swimming in small groups close to the bottom and exploiting the currents. The young hide amidst the algae, drifting with the currents. It measures up to 30 centimetres and is found from Nova Scotia to Argentina.

Queen triggerfish
Balistes vetula

This species swims close to the sea bed busy seeking sea urchins, its favourite prey. It measures up to 60 centimetres and is found from Massachusetts to Brazil.

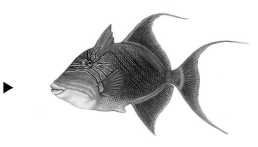

▶

Black durgon
Melichthys niger

◀ This tends to form small groups stationed along the outer slope of the reef down to 60 metres and feeding on large planktonic organisms and algae. It measures up to 50 centimetres and is found in seas around the tropics.

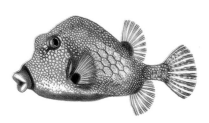

Scrawled filefish
Aluteres scriptus

This swims alone both in lagoons and on the outer reef from where it swims out to open waters. It also feeds on fire corals. It measures up to 1.1 metres and is found in the seas around the tropics.

▶

Smooth trunkfish
Lactophrys triqueter

◀ Normally solitary, this fish sometimes gathers in small groups. It prefers coral beds although it does inspect sandy ones for prey. It measures up to 30 centimetres and is found from Massachusetts to Brazil.

Bandtail puffer
Sphoeroides spengleri

This fish nearly always swims close to the bottom, blending in with the vegetation, detritus or corals. It feeds on the invertebrates found on the sea bed. It measures up to 18 centimetres and is found from Massachusetts to Brazil.

▶

Marbled puffer
Sphoeroides testudineus

◀ This fish prefers coastal bays, rocky formations affected by the tides. It also lives in lagoon water and is rare on reefs. It measures up to 30 centimetres and is found from Bermuda to Brazil.

Branching tube sponge
Pseudoceratina crassa

This sponge is made up of numerous tubes dotted with small protuberances. The tubes originate from a common base and have a large pore at the tip. It measures up to 40 centimetres and is found in the Caribbean.

Azure vase sponge
Callyspongia plicifera

A sponge shaped like a hollow vase with the external surface made up of numerous raised circumvolutional folds with a fluorescent colouring, it grows alone or in small groups. It measures up to 50 centimetres and is found in the Caribbean.

Jellyfish
Cassiopea frondosa

This jellyfish is easily identified by the habit of swimming upside down with its tentacles pointing upwards. It is yellowy brown in colour and is found in the Caribbean.

Brain coral
Colpophyllia natans

This forms large rounded masses, the surface decorated with circumvolute raised formations. The polyps open at night. It measures up to 2 metres and is found from Florida to Venezuela.

Leaf alga
Halimeda sp.

This is one of the most common types of algae found on coral reefs. Sometimes its calcified segments help to compact the reef. It measures up to 20-30 centimetres and is found in seas near the tropics and in temperate waters.

Stove-pipe sponge
Aplysina archeri

This sponge is composed of long hollow tubes originating from a common base. The walls are thin and soft to touch. It appears as isolated colonies, measures up to 1.7 metres and is found in the Caribbean.

Touch-me-not sponge
Neofibularia nolimetangere

A browny coloured sponge, massive and of varying shape. The external surface is similar to a thick felt. If touched it will cause sharp pains. Treat with vinegar. It measures up to 1 metres and is found in the Caribbean.

Star coral
Montastrea annularis

Colonies having a varying appearance from massive to leafy, depending on the habitat. The corallites are very close to each other and similar to small cones. It measures up to 3 metres and is found from Florida to Brazil.

Finger coral
Porites porites

◀ This forms large irregular finger-like ramifications. The external surface is smooth with deep-set corallites. The polyps are open also during the day. It measures up to 1 metres and is found from Florida to Brazil.

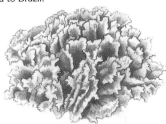

Lettuce coral
Agaricia tenuifolia

The colonies are similar to laminar-like formations gathered together. The surface has raised horizontal ribbing. It measures up to 3 metres and is found from Florida to Brazil. ▶

Staghorn acropore
Acropora palmata

◀ These colonies have very apparent but flattened ramifications. The surface is dotted with small tubular corallites and will break easily if knocked. It measures up to 3.5 metres and is found in the Caribbean.

▶

Gorgonian
Gorgonia ventalina

Gorgonians forming large fans of sizeable ramifications connected to each other by more compact and thinner branches. Usually purple in colour, it measures up to 2 metres and is found in the Caribbean.

Black bush coral
Anthipathes "salix"

◀ This forms large bush colonies with numerous thin ramifications. It grows in poorly illuminated areas and at depths of more than 20 metres. It measures up to 3.5 metres and is found in the Caribbean.

Sea plume
Pseudopterogorgia sp.

Colonies consisting in well-developed ramifications, similar to feathers and forming thick bushes. Generally purple in colour, it measures up to 2 metres and is found in the Caribbean. ▶

Giant anemone
Condilactys gigantea

◀ An anemone with long whitish tentacles terminating in a purple-pink protuberance. It stings slightly, measures up to 30 centimetres and is found in the Caribbean.

Scarlet cleaner prawn
Lysmata grabhami

A cleaner prawn living in sponges from which it allows long white antenna to protrude. It is identified by its red and white stripes, measures up to 6 centimetres and is found in the Caribbean. ▶

Red snapping shrimp
Alpheus armatus

◀ The largest chela can be snapped closed to produce an easily heard sound characteristic of the Alfeidae. Having red and white antennae, it measures up to 6 centimetres and is found in the Caribbean.

Blue crab
Callinectes sp.

The shell is characterized by distinct side spikes; the last rear limbs are flattened and suitable for swimming. It measures up to 20 centimetres and is found from North Carolina to Brazil. ▶

Queen conch
Strombus gigas

◀ This large mollusc has a well-developed shell with a bright pink aperture. It prefers sandy beds around reefs, measures up to 35 centimetres and is found from Florida to Venezuela.

Spotted cyphoma
Ciphoma macgintyi

This mollusc has a white shell but this is not always visible as it is covered by the mantle dotted with round dark spots. It lives on gorgonians, measures up to 3 centimetres and is found in the Caribbean. ▶

Flamingo tongue
Ciphoma gibbosum

◀ The reddish shell of this mollusc is covered with a pink-orange spotted mantle. Living and feeding on gorgonians, it measures up to 3 centimetres and is found in the Caribbean.

Rough fileclam
Lima scabra

This bivalve molusc has a bright red mantle and long tentacles. If disturbed it may flee, opening and closing its valves. It measures up to 7.5 centimetres and is found in the Caribbean. ▶